D1591299

Loving Well

The Key to Satisfying and Joyful Relationships

Also by Erin Leonard

Adolescents with HIV, Depression and Adherence in Adolescents with HIV. Cambria Press 2008

Emotional Terrorism, Breaking the Chains of a Toxic Relationship. Green Dragon Books 2014

The Battle Against Juvenile Bullying: The Plague of Child and Teen Bullying and How to Stop It. Anaphora Literary Press 2015

Reviews of Emotional Terrorism

Dr. Leonard does a wonderful job providing real life examples to help you determine whether you are a victim of emotional terrorism. Emotional terrorism exists in all different relationships, not just intimate ones. This book changed my life! I am now able to identify emotional terrorists keeping my life free of any emotional terrorism. I recommend this book to everyone.   —Sarah Gliss

The best book on the subject of projection and character pathology. If you want to end the confusion you experience when around certain individuals, this book will instruct and guide you through the lose/lose situations these people create in your life and prevent further misery. Do yourself a favor and get educated on this subject matter.   —Kevin Bartlett

A great read and reference for someone who is or has been in a relationship which has left them feeling worthless or less than. Also, a great reference for parents of children and/or adolescents who might be dealing with the aftermath of bullying by an individual or group. Not only does this book give a clear definition of Projective Identification, seemingly the root of most bullying today, but also checklists to determine if this toxic pattern is current in the readers life.   —Nicole Preston

What a truly amazing book!! If you have ever wondered why some relationships are just "off" and are left feeling inadequate in some way, then this book is for you. The way in which the author carries you on a journey using such powerful real life case studies is a true testament to the importance of this subject. You have written an incredible book, and it is going to have a huge impact on people's lives!!!   —Jennifer Flynn

Loving Well

The Key to Satisfying and Joyful Relationships

Dr. Erin K Leonard

Green Dragon Books
Palm Beach, FL
USA

LOVING WELL
The Key to Satisfying and Joyful Relationships
A Green Dragon Publishing Group Publication

© 2016 Green Dragon Books
First Edition

No part of this book may be reproduced or transmitted in any form or by any means, electronic or mechanical, including photocopying, recording, or by any information storage and retrieval system, without written permission from the publisher. For information, address Green Dragon Books ™.

Green Dragon is a trademark of Green Dragon Books ™, consisting of a special identifiable green and unique dragon which is expressingly individual to the publisher. This work is registered with the U.S. Patent and Trademark Office and in other countries.

Green Dragon Books, LLC
2875 S. Ocean Blvd., Ste 200
Palm Beach, FL 33480
info@greendragonbooks.com
www.greendragonbooks.com

Printed in the United States of America and the United Kingdom

ISBN Paperback 9781623860240
ISBN e-Book 9781623860295

Library of Congress Control Number: 2016930640

Table of Contents

Table of Contents

Acknowledgments

This book would not be a reality without my publisher, Gary Wilson, and Green Dragon Books. The support and positive energy I received from Gary and Green Dragon kept my thoughts and fingers inspired.

To my children, Mary and Kenny. You two are the greatest joy in my life. Not much would have meaning without you.

To my mom and dad. My mom taught me how to love, and my dad taught me how to fight for it.

To Andre, my pup. Thanks for being my writing companion.

Introduction

Currently, the divorce rate is over 50% and steadily increasing. Almost everyone these days suffers from anxiety and depression, and not many people in committed relationships are having consistent physical intimacy. Why? Because emotional closeness has been lost. Emotional closeness with someone alleviates depression and anxiety. It leads to satisfying physical intimacy, and it sustains joy, trust, and satisfaction in a person's life. It also produces secure and unanxious children. A large portion of the population is emotionally unevolved, which means, they are less capable of sustaining emotional closeness in their relationships. If you lack emotional closeness in your current relationship, this book will inform you on how to get the love and closeness back before it is lost forever. If you are dating and thinking about making a commitment, this book will ensure you are selecting an emotionally available partner, as well as explain what emotional closeness is, and how to get it and keep it. If you are a parent feeling estranged from your child, this book will help you get the bond back.

CHAPTER 1

The Mismatch

Opposites attract. In most cases, people are attracted to a partner who seems strong in areas where they feel weak. What initially draws people to each other is also what drives them apart, and in many cases, attributes are misjudged. For example, narcissism is often mistaken for confidence. A need for power is often misperceived as ambition, and sympathy is often confused with empathy. In many cases, people set out to create a certain impression, yet, once they get comfortable, their true nature takes over. Love is blind, and the price is high. The sensitive and compassionate get stuck with the detached and selfish. The emotionally evolved marry the emotionally unevolved, and the mismatch in emotional compatibility causes distance and pain in the relationship. But there is help. Understanding how and why this mismatch happens, and how to remedy it, is the goal.

When two people in a relationship are emotionally evolved, emotional closeness is maintained. Both individuals experience and reciprocate empathy, understanding, support, fun, and joy in the relationship. Experiencing new things, joining and sharing in one another's interests and resolving conflict through compromise, accountability, insight, and empathy, solidifies the closeness and continually furthers the couple's emotional evolution. Fights are resolved and considered learning moments. Trust is maintained, and feelings are respected, which leaves little room for resentment or disdain.

The opposite is true when an emotionally evolved person is in a relationship with an unevolved person. Because an emotionally unevolved person is less capable of genuine emotional closeness, the misunderstandings, lack of empathy, and sometimes mistreatment of their partner, creates emotional isolation, anger, distrust, and loneliness in the relationship. The crime in this situation is that it not only traps and discourages the emotionally evolved person from being themselves and experiencing the delight and comfort of the emotional closeness they are capable of, but it sometimes prevents them from continuing to grow and share their gifts with the world. In plain words, the unevolved person can drain the emotionally evolved person of their essence if the situation is not remedied.

Identifying whether someone is emotionally unevolved or emotionally evolved is exceedingly difficult—even for a psychologist. This book hopes to elucidate the emotionally unevolved and the emotionally evolved through explicit descriptions and examples. A general description of both will be provided before going into the specific details so you can decide if these examples resonate with you and you want to know more. My hope is that this book frees the emotionally evolved individual from believing they are the problem when it is actually their partner who needs some help. Also, it is important to note that the differences in evolvement are fundamental and characterological differences. If a person is truly emotionally unevolved, there is a chance they can change, as will be explained, but it takes commitment and motivation. Also, a large proportion of emotionally unevolved people use a fairly pathological defense mechanism, which can result in emotional violence.

Distinguishing between someone who is emotionally unevolved, but is capable of evolution, and someone who is pathologically unevolved is critical as well.

Although an emotionally evolved person has heard the remarks, "You think too much," or "You over analyze," these criticisms are produced by someone who lacks the ability to be self-reflective and insightful about their patterns of relating to others. In other words, they don't care to think about how they impact others. They are mainly consumed with themselves, what they want, and what they like. Unevolved people love to judge and condemn others for anything they deem inappropriate but are unable to judge or look at themselves in the relationship. An unevolved person believes their partner is wrong, emotional and irrational. Often, they believe this so emphatically that they have their emotionally evolved partner believing it. The one exception to this rule, of course, is when their back is against the wall. An example is when their partner puts their foot down and refuses to accept the mistreatment—possibly considering ending the relationship. At this juncture, the unevolved person will wrestle up an apology. It is an insincere apology because they fundamentally believe they did nothing wrong in the first place and were only apologizing to keep their mate from leaving. The problem with this type of an apology is that it is inauthentic, and the same behavior they are apologizing for is immediately resurrected.

The hallmarks of an evolved person are unequivocal. An evolved person believes they have issues. They are sensitive, emotional, and often take responsibility for things that are not their fault, just to end the conflict or save someone else from feeling bad. They feel shame, remorse, will say sorry, and can understand someone else's perspective and opinion even though it differs from their own. They have a creative streak. They feel deeply about the plight of others. Most evolved people appreciate children, dogs, and the elderly. They stand up for the disenfranchised. In their close relationships, they admit fault and own their part in things that went wrong, apologize, and change the behaviors they realize are selfish, often blaming themselves instead of their partner. The final sign of an evolved person is they are ashamed of their anger, despite its justification in many situations.

If you are an unevolved person, this book might not make sense to you, but if you are an evolved person, it resonates deeper than a number of things you have probably read in the past. And the mission of this book is to help the reader identify whether their partner is evolved or unevolved because this will dictate the appropriate course of action. Unevolved people are less capable of emotional closeness because they lack the capacity for empathy (not sympathy, which is confusing, and will be elucidated in a later discussion), insight, and personal accountability within the relationship. For these reasons, they do not mature emotionally. They remain unevolved for most of their lives. An evolved, person, however, because they are insightful, empathic and personally accountable, continue to grow and evolve until they die. Also, an evolved person longs for emotional closeness, whereas an emotionally unevolved person could care less about emotional closeness as long as they are being gratified superficially. Because the evolved person and an unevolved person function on two entirely different emotional and characterological levels, they will inevitably grow apart quickly and this gap continues to widen in time.

One tricky element in deciphering whether your partner is evolved or unevolved is that an emotionally unevolved person is often two-faced. So, when they are with people they want to impress, they are charming, giving, and sympathetic. They revert to who they are once they believe they have roped in the person. The term "roped in" can have several meanings:

1) they have isolated you from friends and family,
2) put a ring on your finger,
3) manipulated you, so you are dependent on them, or,
4) the worst offense, have gotten you to believe you are inferior in some ways and need them to survive.

An equally deceptive phenomenon about unevolved people is they seem to be larger than life in some respects. They have an air of confidence about them. However!—This is not actually confidence; it is narcissism. Unevolved people have fragile egos and, thus, compensate with narcissism and arrogance. They also believe their opinion is the only opinion that matters and that their way is absolutely the right way and the only way. To them, any contradictory notion or plan is wrong and deserves to be criticized. They regard themselves as superior to most others and, therefore, entitled to judge and criticize others. Often, they spend time talking behind someone else's back. The major exception to this is, of course, occurs when they encounter someone more powerful—Instantly they change into a subservient "brown-noser."

Although these are surface descriptions meant to quickly give you an idea of what you should be looking for, the deeper psychological structure of both the evolved and unevolved personalities will be elucidated, to fully explain the differences. Once the deeper nuances of each personality structure are understood, it is easier to consider and help a partner develop the capabilities they need to be emotionally close. Before delving into these deeper details, however, it is important to realize that the qualities we use to attribute readily to good character, actually, have little to do with character or emotional availability.

For example, your mate has a good job and is financially stable or is in school trying to better himself. These are admirable qualities, but many narcissists have good jobs. A good job does not equate to good character. Frequently, I hear the phrase, "she comes from a good family"—meaning a non-divorced, affluent family. Again, I know many emotionally available individuals who came from divorced or single-parent homes, and I see many personality disordered individuals whose parents are affluent and have been married for 40 years. Again, there is no correlation between married parents and good character. Lastly, common interests are often deemed essential to a healthy relationship. "We both love to play golf and go to movies." While these things can set the stage for fun and closeness, they do not guarantee it.

Take, for example, Jules and Eddie. Both love to play golf, yet, because of the underlying hostility in their relationship, their golf outings would quickly turn ugly. Eddie would say something insensitive to Jules, which would hurt Jules feelings. She would explain to Eddie why she felt hurt, but he would tell her she was "oversensitive" and "crazy." Jules, distraught and upset, would miss shots, and loose her ball and Eddie would leave her behind while he continued. Eventually, Jules would throw in the towel and head back to the clubhouse miserable. Eddie would return to the clubhouse and act as though nothing had happened, which dismissed Jules feelings and compounded the insult, thus, driving more distance between Jules and Eddie.

An additional example is Betty and Hank. When they began dating, they loved to watch movies together, but after dating for a while, Betty decided she did not want to watch dramas anymore. She declined every movie Hank suggested and demanded they watch a horror movie. Hank, who has a weak stomach, reluctantly complied and is miserable for most of the movie. Eventually, Hank retires early, leaving Betty to watch it by herself, thus, increasing the emotional distance. In essence, enjoying the same activities is useless if you don't appreciate and respect each other.

The same is true for the superficial aspects of someone. You might like that the person you are dating is educated and has a good job, but that has no bearing on whether this person is selfless, compassionate, and capable of emotional closeness. It may mean they work hard and are intelligent, but it has no relevance to their emotional health. For example, a financially stable person may be financially stable because they are selfish and stingy. Superficial qualities do not equate to good character. They might point in that direction, but it is necessary to look deeper.

Even the qualities which we feel genuinely exude character in an individual, such as a sense of humor and kindness, need to be examined carefully. An unevolved person exhibits kindness in the name of impressing others and not as a genuine and heartfelt gesture. Away from an audience, this selfless gesture evaporates and is replaced by a self-centered preoccupation. For example, because an unevolved person enjoys being the center attention, they often get involved in drama so they can be the "hero." This involvement is only in the name of gaining favorable public opinion, similar to a politician kissing a baby, or a celebrity advertising their charity. But, behind closed doors, they are frequently cold and humorless.—Yet, that is where you will be with them, behind closed doors.

Let's utilize a non-romantic example. After Anne's husband had passed away from cancer, her neighbors, Beth and Emily wanted to help Anne and her children during their time of grief. Beth immediately delegated herself in charge of sending the group emails, organizing dinners to be brought over, and car pools to help Anne's kids. She took every opportunity to mention her involvement to everyone she encountered. Emily was the friend that helped with Anne's dogs every morning at six a.m. and cleaned Anne's house when Anne was out—never mentioning her good deeds to anyone. Emily displayed authentic kindness and compassion. Beth displayed sympathy to garner admiration from others. She used her friend's hardship to further her public persona. Emily exhibited genuine empathy because she related to her friend's pain and wanted to lighten Anne's burden without needing or wanting any acknowledgment for her deeds.

Displaying sympathy or doing something kind to make a good impression in front of others, is, actually, the opposite of kind. Advertising your good deed is self-serving. In essence, when someone uses someone else's misfortune or heartache to further their standing in the community, they are emotionally unevolved. When someone sacrifices something important to them, whether it be time, money, or energy, and expects nothing in return, they are displaying genuine empathy and kindness. Anyone can exhibit sympathy. Feeling sorry for someone requires no sacrifice or emotional investment. Empathy, however, is a different ball game.

The canyon between empathy and sympathy is expansive. Yet, many people do not understand the difference. As recently stated, it is easy to do something nice for someone else when you know it will bring you favorable attention. Sacrificing your energy to help and understand someone else, without a return on this investment, is empathy. Empathy can only occur when one human being perceives another human being as equal. Essentially, when someone values humanity, they have the capacity for empathy. When someone views people as having value only because of a superficial quality like money, power, or social status, they are emotionally unevolved. For example, I have heard several emotionally unevolved people refer to others as "high on the food chain," equating someone's worth as a human being with their ability to garner money or power. These are the people who view people without money or power as unimportant and not worth their time or attention. These people often treat wait staff, or servers at restaurants, very rudely and without common courtesy or respect. Because they devalue people without money or power, they often perceive ordinary people as lower than themselves and less worthy, often treating people disrespectfully and hatefully. These people commonly objectify and dehumanize others, frequently calling them derogatory names.

For example, they refer to women as sluts, bitches, or whores. Men are often called, losers, or fags. Ethnicities are blankly referred to by racist terms as are homosexuals. Poor people are not acknowledged because they are the lowest species on the "food chain" according to an emotionally unevolved individual. When people are objectified and dehumanized, it is impossible to have empathy for them. Because of this world perception, unevolved people have very little empathy for others, often believing people deserve whatever misfortune they encounter, and inflicting violence on others as if it's their right. This lack of empathy for others is the number one hallmark of an emotionally unevolved individual.

On the other hand, a person who actually cares about how other people feel, regardless of whether they have money or power, and perceives human beings as equal because of their human core, is truly empathic. It is impossible to have empathy if you do not perceive humanness as the most valuable quality of an individual. When you value a person's humanness over any other quality, you relate to them as an equal. And as an equal, you can try and put yourself in another's shoes. Sacrificing your happiness for a moment, you attempt to feel the other person's pain so you can understand it and be with them, so they are not alone with their pain. Empathy is one of the most unselfish acts in which a human being can participate. Jesus, Mother Teresa, Gandhi, Martin Luther King, and Luis Zamparini are examples of people with enormous capacities for empathy.

Another factor distinguishing the emotionally evolved from the unevolved is the tendency to seek revenge or retribution due to feeling wronged personally. This behavior is often referred to as being passive aggressiveness and aggressive. The belief that you are entitled to hurt or actively or destroy someone, because you feel they have personally wronged you, is primitive, immature, and in extreme cases dangerous. An emotionally evolved individual may be angry and upset about an interaction, but they do not fixate on "getting back" at this individual. They usually talk about their feelings, allow themselves to be sad and mad for a bit, and move on with their lives. If they remain stuck with negative feelings about the person, they do not act on them by attempting to thwart or sabotage the other person in a vindictive manner as an emotionally unevolved person would.

Believing you are a victim plays into the belief that seeking revenge is your right. As childish as it seems, unevolved adults like to blame other people for their mistakes instead of taking responsibility for them. So, a husband who mistreats his wife continually, and then cries to his children, "Your mom left me. I'm all alone. She destroyed my life," is an example of an adult playing the victim. Another example includes an individual who isn't able to excel at his or her job because of lack of effort, and then complains and blames the person that got the promotion for "stealing their job." These sentiments are simple examples of the flawed thinking of emotionally unevolved individuals. Because they believe they are the victim, they are not able to take responsibility for their mistakes or mistreatment of others, and because they are unable to take responsibility for their actions, they repeat them over and over. A person is only able to change and grow if they recognize their shortcomings. Blaming others prevents any sort of emotional growth. Unevolved people are stuck repeating the same mistakes in their relationships continually. Thus, the individual who is mistreated or hurt in the relationship stops mentioning the pain and frustration because they either get blamed for it, or they get a superficial apology, and they are treated the same way day in and day out for years. This type of disconnect breeds emotional distance and hostility. This tendency to blame your partner instead of understanding and taking responsibility for your part in the conflict can wreak havoc in a relationship.

In addition, an unevolved personality also plays the victim to escape responsibilities. For example, they might complain about working long hours to excuse themselves from any responsibility for the kids or with an activity that is important to their partner. An evolved personality, on the other hand, is usually prepared to dig in and do whatever it takes to meet work, parental, and personal responsibilities. They are apt to take responsibility for most things in their life. An unevolved person shirks the duties they view as beneath them by feigning hardship.

Another significant difference between an unevolved person and evolved person is the fluidity of their perspectives and opinions. An evolved person enjoys learning from others and of their opinions, and is open to new perspectives—and this is the important part—is open to them even if they conflict with their perspective and opinion. It might take a little while, but eventually, they understand and are interested in this different train of thought. They enjoy learning about other cultures and people. They are interested in what "makes people tick," looking for the deeper motivations and feelings of others to better understand them.

An emotionally unevolved person, however, usually considers no other opinion but their own. They believe their opinion is the only right opinion, and they reject and make fun of others with a different view. The same is true for their perspective. Only able to see life from their perspective, they immediately reject and scoff at any offering of a different viewpoint. In other words, they believe their way is the only way and any other way is wrong.

Open minded, curious, and deep, an evolved person continually attempts to understand and see things from different perspectives, which makes them far less judgmental. An unevolved person continually judges and puts others down; sometimes it is so pervasive that it becomes this person's source of entertainment—gossip and talking negatively about others.

Due to the concrete, or black and white, thinking of an emotionally unevolved individual, often they gravitate towards religion because religion sometimes offers a black and white view of life. For example, homosexuality is wrong. Divorce is wrong. Abortion is wrong. These are absolutes, which make them black and white thoughts. A judgment is levied in a concrete fashion without attempting to understand a deeper meaning of each particular situation. In addition, often religion provides people with the idea that if they think this way, they are morally superior and more deserving of good things than others. Instead of compassion, this black and white, morally superior attitude perpetuates hate for fellow human beings instead of love.

Despite the black and white nature of their thinking, emotionally unevolved people can be evolved intellectually. They can be exceedingly bright, and are often good at jobs which require an analytic and calculating mind. Their intellect often allows them to succeed and become very accomplished. Because of their rigidity of thought, inflexibility, and criticism of others, they make their subordinates, and sometimes co-coworkers continually anxious and worried. Often they are workplace bullies, using their power to inflate their ego by zapping others. The deep insecurities which compel them to constantly put down others in order secure their own power are so fundamental that they have no awareness of them. They sincerely believe themselves to be superior to others. Unfortunately, some of the world's most maniacal and evil leaders have suffered from this exact plight. Napoleon, Hitler, Ben Laden, etc., are all men who have been unable to tolerate their shortcomings, so they project them onto the world and feel entitled to destroy others. We elect a leader or assign someone power because we believe they have given us a direction and unified people. Yet, they have used hate as the adhesive and blame as the excuse. Fear is the next weapon. Purposely destroying their victims publicly, they solidify their absolute power with terror.

Also, an unevolved person will parrot what they believe they should say, but they cannot back it up with their behaviors. So, they say things to make others think they are a good person, but they cannot reinforce it. For example, an unevolved person might tell her partner that she loves who he is and wouldn't change a thing, but the next day berates him for not making more money and for spending too much time with his children. In summary, their actions do not back up their words.

The unevolved personality is also perplexing because they are occasionally nice. Often, they give gifts. Although these are seemingly thoughtful gestures, they are slightly manipulative. The nice personality is resurrected in order to "reel" their partner in and manipulate their partner into trusting them again, so they can control their partner. The gift-giving phenomenon is indicative of the unevolved person's inability to be emotionally close. Their idea of showing love is not through the quality of their interactions, but by giving their partner gifts or by spending money on them. This is not love, not even remotely close to love. An unevolved partner is content with these gestures. However, an evolved partner needs genuine love to feel satisfied and would gladly give up money or material objects for it. Again, the unevolved persona has a Dr. Jekyll and Mr. Hyde type of feel. They are friendly and charming around people they want to impress, but treat others with disrespect and cruelty.

Although a detailed description of an unevolved person's character has been discussed, and the deceptive nature of their personality described, some hallmarks or sure-fire signs of an unevolved individual need to be outlined to condense the information before moving on to the evolved person.

The most important information comes from your interactions and relationship with your partner. One imperative thing to think about is how the two of you deal with conflict. There are a couple of different scenarios which are common with an evolved person and an unevolved person in a relationship together.

The first scenario usually involves one person (A) getting their feelings hurt by the other person, or one person (A) feeling disrespected or mistreated by the other. When person A identifies they are hurt and angry about the situation, does person B dismiss their feelings and tell them they are ridiculous or even insecure or crazy for feeling the way they do? If this is B's continual response to A's feelings—to dismiss A's feelings, reject any idea that they could have done something wrong, and turn it back onto A as if A is the problem, then you might be involved with an emotionally unevolved person. A can attempt to explain calmly why he feels the way he does multiple times, but this falls on B's deaf ears. B believes he is not at fault at all. B makes A feel crazy for even trying to explain, which hurts and angers A more intensely because it is a continual slap in the face to be told your feelings are wrong, and you are crazy. When A becomes increasingly upset, B uses this against A as evidence that A is irrational. A has two choices. The first is to give up, agree with B that she/he is wrong to have felt the way they did, and it is their issue. Yet, this is dangerous because giving up your dignity and allowing someone to disrespect you emotionally and psychologically is an awful position to be in. A's second choice is to continue to explain why their feelings were hurt, continuing the vicious cycle of B deflecting any responsibility and blaming A, which makes A seem like she wants to fight continually, or that A is constantly picking on B, which is the opposite of what is actually happening.

This is an important example because it exemplifies the characteristics of an unevolved person:

1) B lacks empathy for A. B cannot put himself in A's shoes, or even for a moment, consider how A feels.
2) B is unable to take responsibility for himself in the relationship. B won't even entertain the idea that he had a part in the conflict.
3) B externalizes blame. He blames A for the situation.
4) B plays the victim. B complains that he has been the one hurt in the scenario, and he is the victim of A's irrationality.

A second scenario includes disputes about who "gets their way." In most situations, the evolved person (A) is laid back, open minded, and open to doing things another person's way, because they are usually open to other's perspectives, and are flexible, and amenable to trying new things. A is usually good at compromising and finding a middle ground. B, the unevolved person, is fairly rigid and demanding that things are done his way. If things aren't done his way, he often quits or refuses to do anything. B is far less open to trying something that A wants to do and often puts it down. Of course, when A does feel passionate about getting her way for some reason, there is conflict. B will sometimes give in, but frequently will attempt to sabotage underhandedly the plans or A, because B is passive aggressive and vindictive in nature. A is then disappointed, and B takes the opportunity to gloat. B continues to bring up this situation in the future to deter A from ever insisting they do things her way once in a while.

This scenario also exemplifies the character of an unevolved person:

1. They are self-centered and demanding. It is their way or the highway.
2. When they do not get their way, they are vindictive and try to thwart or sabotage their partner in order to "get back at them."
3. B is threatened by A's interest in new and interesting things because it takes them away from B's control, so they ridicule or criticize the new things A wants to try.

In essence, if these are typical scenarios in your relationship, and you resonate with how A feels, there is a strong chance your partner is unevolved emotionally. Because the core character is entirely different between the evolved and unevolved, it is going to take work to achieve emotional closeness. If your partner lacks motivation or openness for this endeavor, ending the relationship may be an important consideration.

There has been much discussion and detail about unevolved individuals and the differences between an unevolved person and an evolved person, but what are the nuances and details of an evolved personality? Hopefully, the next discussion will elucidate this. As previously alluded to, an emotionally evolved person is sensitive, compassionate, empathic, and insecure. The last adjective doesn't seem to fit with the prior adjectives, but it is true. Because an emotionally evolved person is self-reflective and capable of insight, they are critical of themselves, which sometimes causes them to feel insecure and less worthwhile than others. It is this ability to analyze their interactions, identify their shortcomings, and try to improve them, which continually makes them capable of emotional evolution. In fact, many emotionally available people so readily take responsibility for their flaws, that they will often assume responsibility for someone else's mistake as well, just to protect the other person from pain or embarrassment.

Moreover, because they are continually reflecting on their short-comings, they are a very humble lot. They do not believe they are better than anyone else and are quick to see the humanness in others. They are the opposite of narcissistic, which sometimes has them also believing that they do have issues because they see others around them as more confident and more capable. What they don't realize is that it is narcissism, vanity, and the inflated egos of emotionally unevolved personalities that they are witnessing, not true confidence.

Because they are deeply sensitive, emotionally evolved individuals often use their emotional intelligence to excel at their jobs, artistic endeavors, or creative hobbies. They are strong at connecting with others. Once in a while, an emotionally evolved person will unknowingly get involved with a host of emotionally unevolved people, and when this happens, the emotionally evolved person's kindness and sensitivity is often used against them.

Emotionally evolved people are easily and readily taken advantage of and bullied by the emotionally unevolved, and occasionally will feel so used and emotionally beat up that they start to disengage. At its worst, the emotionally evolved will isolate themselves and shy away from making new friends or doing anything social. They have been too hurt. A similar phenomenon occurs when they are in a relationship with an emotionally unevolved person. They are frequently mistreated, taken advantage of, hurt, and persuaded into believing they deserve to be treated as such because they are the problem.

Often this occurs because most emotionally unevolved people are jealous of emotionally evolved people. It's almost like they sense the depth and breadth of an emotionally evolved person's character and unconsciously recognize that they are not built that way. Frequently, this leads to jealousy which motivates the unevolved individual to try and dominate and control the emotionally evolved person, because they are jealous and threatened. Also, because emotionally evolved people are generally happy, and emotionally unevolved people are fundamentally unhappy, the unevolved are, again, jealous of the evolved. This jealousy is utterly unrecognizable to the evolved person, which is yet another confusing factor contributing to this dynamic.

Because of their character, an emotionally evolved person is usually humble and self-effacing. They would not consider the possibility that someone might be jealous of them, so they are blind to this dynamic. They are blind and, then, blindsided when the unevolved person does something hurtful, disloyal, and underhanded. The difficulty with this situation is a result of the unevolved person taking no responsibility for their behavior in the relationship—blaming most things on their partner. The evolved person is only left with one conclusion—that somehow they deserve this treatment, especially if multiple unevolved individuals have contributed to this belief. It is very difficult for them to consider it is not them and it is, actually, the other person at fault.

Because emotionally evolved people have a deep and complicated emotional capacity, they feel the injustice in their bones. They may be manipulated into thinking that their partner's problems and the issues in the relationship are their fault, but deep down, they know that something is very wrong. When the time comes to accept that, they are usually able to gather enough strength to confront their partner, or end the relationship.

Perhaps this is why emotionally evolved individuals have an enormous capacity for empathy. Because they, themselves, have been stripped of their dignity, and so they empathize with the less fortunate, the marginalized, the disenfranchised, and the bullied. Possibly, it's is also because they have a strong self-esteem. This strength allows them to feel the pain of others in order to better understand and help them. An intense capacity for empathy is a bit like a super power.

Take, for example, Luis Zamperini, Olympic runner, war hero, and humanitarian. He was not a hero because he was big and strong. He was a hero because of his character. His capacity for empathy was so intense; it qualified him as supernatural. He sacrificed his needs on a lifeboat in the middle of the Pacific Ocean to try and save his fellow soldiers. In a Japanese POW camp, sick with dysentery, dehydration, and starvation, he agreed to race against the Japanese Olympic runner, who was in top physical condition, in order to salvage the dignity that was stripped from his fellow soldiers. Equipped with the knowledge that if he won the race, which wasn't physically possible, he would return dignity, humanness and hope to his fellow camp mates who were stripped of everything that made them human. Despite the awareness that a victory would mean he would be beaten within an inch of his life, he ran. His character and capacity for empathy transcended his physical capabilities and his body fueled by his spirit trumped his opponents. He won, and his friends hung on.

The same character and capacity for empathy that allowed him to salvage his and his campmates' spirit, empowered him to forgive his torturer later in life. Unlike someone with a weak self-esteem and a fragile ego, he did not seek revenge or vindication. He forgave. In time, he forgave.

When someone intentionally humiliates someone else, degrades them, and does not respect how the other person feels, it has a dehumanizing effect, which is extremely painful. However, an emotionally evolved person has difficulty allowing the awareness that their partner is pathological to reach full consciousness for several reasons. The first is because they are trusting and loving human beings, who want to see the good in people. It is easier for them to blame themselves than to believe someone they love and trust is manipulative and mean.

The second reason is that emotionally evolved people are ashamed of their own anger. Anger is a negative emotion which is uncomfortable for an emotionally evolved person because it contradicts their happy and good natured character. Thirdly, the depth and breadth of emotions are sophisticated in an emotionally evolved person. When an emotionally evolved person feels joy, they feel it intensely. When they feel empathy, they feel it intensely. When they feel grief, they feel it intensely. And when they feel anger, they feel it intensely.

Finally, because they are stripped of their dignity when they are involved in a relationship with an unevolved person, the anger they feel is profound. Because they are uncomfortable and ashamed of their anger, regardless of whether it is warranted or not, they immediately become ashamed of their angry response, quickly surrender, and take responsibility for the situation. The problem is that their partner never takes responsibility for their part, so the only person admitting fault is the person that was victimized in the first place. If an unevolved person is angered, they not only express their anger inappropriately but become vindictive and passive aggressive. Polar opposite responses to the experience of anger.

An additional quality shared among emotionally evolved people is resilience. They are tough, yet, they don't realize they are tough because this "take it on the chin" attitude is second nature to them. They endure hardship quietly and work diligently to make things better. After mistakes or disappointments, they search for their part in the situation and desperately try to avoid making that mistake again. They have a high emotional pain tolerance, so to speak, and can endure hardship if it benefits someone they love. In other words, they are selfless. The unevolved person, on the other hand, calls attention to any act they can frame as selfless, and they feign physical and emotional hardship every opportunity they can to manipulate others. This "victim stance" is just another way for them to escape personal accountability for themselves.

The evolved person is not a saint, by any stretch. They are usually fun-loving and spontaneous, which can sometimes get them into trouble. Because they enjoy life and are open to trying new things, they often take time for themselves and have a nice way of balancing "me time" and their commitments to others. This balance, however, is frequently thrown off when they are in a relationship with an unevolved individual because the unevolved individual is jealous of the evolved person's happiness and enjoyment if it doesn't involve them. Often, they attempt to sabotage the evolved person's participation in activities or interests.

A final quality of an emotional evolved person is their emotional complexity and depth. They have an intense understanding and interest in other human beings. Curious about different cultures and customs, they have a keen ability to see the humanness in others, even if they are from a foreign land or culture.

Identity

Although the characteristics of both the evolved personality and the unevolved personality have been articulated, a deeper explanation of both identities is necessary. An evolved person's identity is fairly consolidated. Their identity, which can also be understood as their ego or self-esteem, is strong enough to withstand negative feedback. Experiencing this negative feedback is painful, but an evolved person is able to process it and use it to grow and evolve. They are capable of self-reflection and self-analysis, which require a strong identity. Although it hurts, they continually look at their flaws in order to try to and improve. Often they accept responsibility because they're strong enough to bare the discomfit that accompanies it. In essence, if an evolved person's identity had a structure, it would probably be made of wood. So, when a rock is thrown at it, it might nick the wood and maybe even leave a notch, but it would not destroy the structure.

An unevolved person's identity is fragile. As already stated, they compensate for a weak identity with narcissism. If their identity had a structure, it would be made of glass. So, if a rock is hurled at it, the structure would shatter. This explains why an unevolved person has to defend and deflect anything that comes at it. If blame and shame are not deflected and projected out, their identity would shatter. They are constantly on the look-out for anything that might come their way, so they can deflect it and attack back. This is why they lack insight and have a difficult time taking responsibility for themselves—because that requires allowing negative data through. It also explains why they continually externalize blame. Moreover, because their weak identity must be protected at all times, they are resistant to understanding someone else's viewpoint if it challenges theirs. When they are forced to take responsibility, they have a number of excuses and justifications for their behavior. Thus, they continue to protect themselves from any tiny ounce of accountability.

The problem occurs when the evolved person and the unevolved person are in an intimate relationship because the unevolved person has a tendency to project and deflect onto to the evolved person, and because the evolved person is self-reflective and accountable, often they absorb the blame and shame. Over time, this process erodes the evolved person's identity and fuels the unevolved person's narcissism.

When an identity is eroded over time, it causes feelings of confusion, shame, depression and anxiety. Reconsolidating a dismantled identity takes time. Depression and anxiety can consume the person unless they begin to recover their identity.

CHAPTER 2

Emotional Closeness

Unfortunately, emotional closeness has not been defined, nor has it been identified as the goal for most romantic relationships, and, or more importantly, the parent and child relationship. Because it is essential in these two types of relationships, both will be included in this discussion.

Emotional closeness must be the goal in these relationships because it allows for empathy, understanding, tolerance, forgiveness, trust, fun, passion, and compromise. Without emotional closeness, hurt, disappointment, loneliness, and resentment rule as the most common emotions in the relationship. Think about every movie, song, novel, and other forms of modern or historical commentary. Most movies, songs, and novels center around the pain of emotional distance in relationships that are supposed to be close or the absolute joy experienced in an emotionally close relationship. Thousands of love songs about "falling in love" are actually about the discovery of emotional closeness with a stranger. When this "in love" feelings disappears, it's because emotional closeness was lost. Heartbreak is, actually, the loss of emotional closeness.

So what is emotional closeness? It's the feeling of being understood. It's the feeling of being respected and valued, and not for your achievements, but for who you are. It's the experience of having your feelings understood and respected. Feelings are the essence of who we are. Our soul, spirit and character are just words that describe the conglomerate of our feelings. Emotions drive every single thing we do, and if we don't respect and honor our partner's emotions or our children's emotions, we are hurting them. Emotions are never wrong. It's what we do with them that is sometimes the problem.

Let's take, for example, jealousy, a normal human emotion. An emotionally healthy person can readily identify their jealousy, admit it, and maybe even laugh about it. "She's a gifted piano player. Gosh, I wish I could play like that. I'm so jealous. Perhaps in another life I'll play like that." An emotionally unhealthy person can't admit they are jealous and acts out feelings of jealousy instead. They might talk negatively about the pianist behind her back, or post a nasty message about her on social media.

Or, in the context of a romantic relationship, one person, Anne, might identify her jealousy about her partner's ex-girlfriend. "Gosh, Lucy is so beautiful and smart. Why did you guys break up? She seems like she has it all. I'm a little jealous." Because Anne identified and verbalized how she felt, her partner has the opportunity to understand her feelings and reassure her that she is equally as pretty and smart AND that Lucy farts in her sleep. An unhealthy partner, on the other hand, might condemn Anne for her jealous feelings and tell her she is insecure. In the first scenario, Anne is honest about her feelings and her partner respects and understands them while also reassuring her. Anne feels close to her mate, and her mate is most likely flattered that Anne is slightly jealous, so emotional closeness is enhanced. In the second scenario, Anne's feelings are not respected. The unhealthy partner conveys to her that her feelings are wrong, and there is something wrong with her, i.e. insecure. This creates emotional distance.

The first step in establishing and maintaining emotional closeness is respecting the other person's feelings—even if you don't agree with them. The following is an additional example using the parent child dyad. A mom is busy working on her presentation, and her daughter, Molly, suddenly appears in the doorway crying and yelling: "I hate school! I hate first grade! I'm not going to first grade!" Molly's mom is annoyed at the interruption and the ugliness of the outburst, and she would like nothing more than to send Molly to her room to calm down—especially since first grade doesn't start for three weeks and her presentation is due the following day, but she gives it more thought and decides she must put Molly's feelings first. So, she sets aside her computer and attempts to be empathic. In a soft and gentle voice, she says, "You are really upset about going into the first grade." Molly, says "Yes! I don't want to go! I'm not going!" Molly's mom again honors Molly's feelings and says, "You are really upset. Tell me what the most upsetting thing about the first grade is?" Molly softens a bit and says, "I don't know who my teacher is, and she might be mean. It might be too hard, and the day might be too long, and I might miss you too much!" Molly's mom hugs her and, again, honors Molly's feelings. She says, "Those are big worries. Very big worries. I get it. I understand. I wouldn't want to go either if I had those worries. Those things are scary," and she takes a few moments to hug Molly and stroke her hair. She then says, "If any of those worries happen honey, I will help you. You will not be alone. I will help you." After a few more moments, she moves from empathy to problem solving. She asks Molly if finding out who her teacher is and meeting her at orientation would help. She also asks if finding out which of her friends were in her class would help. She also reminded Molly that the first grade day was exactly the same length of the kindergarten day, and she mastered that.

The difficulty is that empathy requires emotional sacrifice on the part of the person who is being empathic. Empathy requires a person set aside their own feelings so they can try and understand how someone else feels, which means they must be emotionally evolved. It is much easier and less sacrificial to tell a person they shouldn't feel the way they do or to tell them how to solve their problem. In the Molly example, the logical argument would be to tell Molly that there are no mean teachers at her school and that she aced kindergarten, so it's ridiculous to for her to think first grade would be too hard. Also, the kindergarten day is the same length as the first grade day, and she handles that successfully so she should have no problem with the length of the day. All of these statements are logical, but if they are stated right away, they dismiss and contradict Molly's feelings and communicate to Molly that her feelings are wrong, which leads to three serious long term problems.

The first problem with telling your child they are wrong to feel the way they do immediately detracts from their self-esteem. When a child continually hears that their feelings are wrong, they begin not to trust their feelings. They also begin to be ashamed of their own emotions, because they are told they are wrong. This has grave mental health repercussions for the child.

The second problem is that this is a barrier to emotional closeness between the child and the parent. If a child is constantly told that their feelings are wrong, they will stop coming to the parent with them. They will stop talking to their parent about their feelings, problems, fears, worries, etc. because their parent makes it worse. "She never talks to me. She won't tell me anything," are phrases I continually hear from parents. It's because they have not honored their child's feelings.

Thirdly, if a child does not receive empathy or understanding with their fears and worries, their worries do not dissipate. They linger and intensify until the child is so anxious they don't even understand what they are anxious about. If a child receives empathy, they are able to quickly metabolize their anxiety and move through life with confidence and security.

An important misconception to clarify is that parents believe if they empathize with their child's feelings, they are condoning bad behavior. Not true. A parent can honor their child's feelings while still holding up appropriate consequences, expectations, and discipline. It is as simple as saying something like, "Kevin, I know you're mad and you're disappointed, but it is not ok to throw your backpack."

So, the first step in establishing and sustaining emotional closeness is empathy, respecting and honoring your loved one's feelings—even if you disagree with how they feel. The second step is holding yourself accountable in the relationship. Without each partner taking responsibility for their insensitivities or selfishness in the relationship, angry and hurt feelings linger, and mistrust snowballs.

Let's take the example of Jack and Diane as an example. Diane was nervous about an important presentation for work. Jack was supportive and encouraging the morning of the presentation, and Diane left the house feeling supported. Although initially anxious, Diane pulled off the rather difficult presentation. Afterward, she was relieved, but needed reassurance that the presentation was a success, so she sent the media clip of the presentation to Jack and asked him for his feedback. As the day passed, she anxiously awaited Jack's response. That evening when she got home, she asked Jack if he had time to review the clip. He said no, that although he was off work that day he had been busy with other things. Diane was hurt. She went to bed early that night. The following morning, Diane woke up and felt better. She was sure Jack would give her the feedback she needed when he had time that day, so she went off to work eagerly anticipating his text.

At noon, she texted Jack and asked for his feedback. He said he'd "get to it" by the end of the day. Diane and Jack had dinner plans that evening, so when she didn't hear from Jack, she assumed they would have plenty of time to discuss it at dinner. When she arrived home, Jack was rushing out the door. He had forgotten that he had made plans with a neighbor to build their kid's go kart for the go kart race the following weekend.

Diane was crushed. Angry, disappointed and hurt, she stewed all evening, and when Jack got home, she told Jack she was hurt and angry. Jack was indignant. He told Diane he was busy doing things for their kids and they came first. He also told Diane she should be secure with herself and not be so "oversensitive." Diane was miffed. Jack was so adamant that she started to question herself. Was she so insecure that she needed reassurance about something she should be secure about? Her feelings of anger and hurt lingered, but she also questioned herself and her own judgment.

When personal accountability is deflected, emotional distance is created because hurt and anger linger and eventually turn into resentment and mistrust. If Jack would have simply sat down with Diane and said he was sorry for being inconsiderate and insensitive, Diane's negative feelings would immediately dissipate, and emotional closeness would be restored. In fact, the resolution of conflict might even bring the two closer. Also, Jack would probably try his best not make that mistake again.

This lack of personal accountability can be extremely frustrating, and the person who is on the opposite end spends a great deal of time hurt and angry. Having to continually defend and justify their feelings is exhausting because it falls on deaf ears. Often, they are left with two choices, surrender to the idea that they are oversensitive and insecure as their partner says, or become complacent with the mistreatment. Unfortunately, neither choice is healthy, and the chasm of emotional distance widens.

The deceptive element in this situation is that an unevolved person is able to take responsibility for themselves outside of the relationship because there are consequences for negative behaviors. For example, they can assume responsibility for a mistake at work or with some of their friends because there are checks and balances in these realms, but they won't in their romantic relationship because they believe they hold the power. In essence, they experience the world in very concrete terms. Whether they are aware of it or not, in their eyes, two types of people exist: 1) People who are more powerful than they are (and whom they want to impress), or 2) People who are less powerful than they are. The difference in the way they act around people in these two different categories is drastic. It's almost like a Dr. Jekyll and Mr. Hyde type of personality. Also, the difference in the way they treat people in these two categories is also extreme. So, with people they want to impress they are extremely subservient, and they hold themselves accountable. Yet, they are often rude, arrogant, and insensitive when interacting with people they deem less powerful than they are.

Another nuance important in understanding this dynamic is that unevolved personality is childlike in terms of their fear of consequences or punishment. They hold themselves accountable because they are forced to by bosses, law enforcement figures, their attorney, etc. and they realize if they don't hold themselves accountable there will be significant consequences. Yet, if these consequences we not present, they would feel entitled to do whatever they want. This explains why they feel justified in maintaining their "I'm not wrong—you are" thinking. There are no consequences unless their partner threatens to leave, or if they want something from their partner. At these times, they will insincerely hold themselves accountable to get what they want, but continue the same insensitive behavior immediately after they get what they want.

Unfortunately, because an unevolved person is almost always narcissistic, they view their partner as having a lower value than themselves, which also feeds into their delusion that they are always right, and their partner is always wrong. This can also be confusing because they might flaunt their partner in ways that fuel their own ego. For example, they might brag to other people that their wife is a doctor or that she was a supermodel, but this is to fluff their own ego. They use their partner to look good. As soon as they get home, however, and impressing people is not an option, they continue to mistreat their partner.

A similar dynamic can be witnessed in the parent-child relationship. Often, parents believe they can't admit fault because it will strip them of their authority. This could not be further from the truth. No parent, despite how great of a parent they are, is perfect. Nor are they anywhere near perfect. Admitting a mistake is the first step in **not** repeating it again. In the grand scheme of things, it's our mistakes that allow us grow as people and evolve as human beings—as long as we admit them. Intuitively, children know their parents aren't perfect. Yet, they love their parent despite these imperfections. So when a parent doesn't admit fault in their relationship with their child, they are not fooling the child. The child usually knows. So, they are teaching the child to excuse themselves of accountability. When a parent holds themselves accountable, they are securing the relationship with trust, humility, and hope for a better way next time. These traits are imperative to a child's character, self-esteem, and mental health.

Raising children that can hold themselves accountable is only achieved if their parent models this for them. When the child experiences their parent taking responsibility for themselves in the relationship, they learn how to take responsibility for themselves and then they do it naturally. A parent who tries to teach their child personal accountability through punitive measures instead of allowing their child to experience it, will have a child that blames others, and manipulates in order to escape taking responsibility for their actions because that is what they have experienced in the relationship with their parent.

A second parental fear regarding personal accountability is that doing so automatically excuses the child from any wrongdoing. Not true. If a parent makes a mistake and admits it, they are not instantly excusing the child from accountability. Each person must take responsibility for their part in a negative and dysfunctional interaction. Only then, is there hope that things will be different next time. The same goes for the romantic partnership.

Also, when a parent owns their mistakes, it allows the parent to gain insight into themselves, although sometimes this can be painful. Insight is what helps us evolve and become better people. It is also what allows us to be successful, not only in our relationships but in life.

Let's take the example of Tommy and his mom, Amy. One evening, Amy was attempting to get Tommy and his sister ready to meet friends for dinner, but Tommy wasn't cooperating. He was fussing about the special coin he had misplaced. Amy reassured him that she would help him find it when they returned from dinner, but Tommy would not agree. He continued to carry on crying and yelling about how they needed to find his coin. Amy continued to reassure him and promise that she would help him find it as soon as they returned from dinner. Yet Tommy would not relent. Finally frustrated, Amy grabbed Tommy and said, "Buddy, the world does not revolve around you. We have people waiting for us!" Tommy looked her in the eye and softly responded with, "The world doesn't revolve around you either." Amy was surprised and confused. Her brain working overtime trying to figure out what her son meant. "Do I act like the world revolves around me?" she asked. Tommy said, "Yes, your book." Again, Amy was perplexed, and she put some deep thought into what Tommy was saying, and it hit her. She threw minor fits when she couldn't find something she needed for her book. Amy looked at Tommy and said, "I do throw a fit when I can't find something for my book." Tommy nodded. Amy looked at him and asked, "So, you've learned this from me?" Tommy nodded yes. Amy apologized and said she wouldn't throw any more fits when she couldn't find something for her book. Tommy hugged her said he wouldn't either, and before she knew it, he had his jacket on and was heading for the car—ready to go to dinner.

As parents, we cannot be too busy correcting behavior to miss the deeper communications in the relationship. Moreover, when our child tries to tell us something about ourselves, it's imperative to listen. Tommy gave his mom several hugs that night and told her, "I love you, mom." He felt close to his mom, who was, not only able to hold herself accountable, but help him with his feelings. She did not threaten or punish. She listened. Trust what your child is telling you about yourself.

The Equation for Emotional Closeness:

Empathy
+
Personal Accountability in the Relationship
=
Emotional Closeness

CHAPTER 3

Emotional Distance

Emotional distance has been explained in juxtaposition to emotional closeness, but there are a few additional points. Sympathy is not empathy, and it does not contribute to emotional closeness. It seems nice. And it is, but it is also disempowering. Empathy, as described previously, only occurs when there is equality in the relationship. Thus, when a partner is sympathetic, it can be tricky because it appears to be kind. For example, if someone says to a physically handicapped person, "I feel so sorry that you can't walk—let me carry you up the stairs," they are the hero and the strong and capable being in the interaction, and the physically challenged person is rendered helpless and in need of rescuing. On the other hand, if the person says, "What do you need me to do, so you can get up the stairs?" The person is understanding and compassionate but does not detract from the physically handicapped person's dignity. Now, if there were a fire, I would hope that the physically able person would grab the physically challenged person and take them to safety. However, in everyday situations, it's important for one person to take the time to respect the other person's agency and refrain from being the "rescuer."

The same concept is true for romantic partnerships. If one person relays a difficult or painful situation to their partner, and their partner immediately tells them what to do to fix their problem, it is disempowering. If the partner, on the other hand, tries to understand their partner's feelings and then asks what they can do to help, or asks the partner if specific suggestions would help, they are empowering their partner.

In addition, it is essential for the partner listening to their distressed partner to be empathic. This is a crucial step in supporting and helping the partner that is upset. Although empathy takes a unique mindset and requires the individual set aside their own feelings for a moment in order to try and feel what their partner is feeling, it is critical. After identifying how their partner feels, for example: "You feel incompetent when Gus is around. That's a terrible feeling. I understand. I would feel the same way if I were you."

The key here is being empathic towards your partner when he or she is angry with you, not simply when your partner has an issue outside of your relationship. This can be exceedingly difficult because when someone takes an issue with another person, the person usually instinctively leaps to their own defense. Many times, they try to explain or justify their behaviors. Yet, this contradicts the other person's feelings. Respecting someone's feelings is not an automatic admission of guilt, but it is sure fire sign of empathy, and it will heal whatever it was that hurt your partner.

Take, for example, Katy and Ed. Ed had lunch with his ex-girlfriend while he was seriously involved with Katy, but neglected to tell her of the meeting. Katy, upset and angry, confronted Ed. Ed vehemently argued that he had innocent and honorable motives, and Katy believed him, but her anger and hurt over the situation lingered. She felt herself pulling away from Ed and acting defensive in their interactions. Eventually, Ed realized empathy was necessary in order to put the ugly conflict to rest. He said, "I bet you felt betrayed and hurt when you discovered I had lunch with Chrissy. I'm so sorry I hurt you. That is the last thing I wanted to do. If I were in your place, I would be upset too." Following this empathic statement should, then, be the justification for why the encounter occurred and why Ed wasn't upfront with Katy. So, empathy first, explanation second. Having empathy for your partner is not an admission of fault or guilt, but is necessary to mend a rift between you and your partner and move forward happily instead of with doubt and distrust.

Also, when there is emotional distance in the relationship, the evolved person will feel it much more so than the unevolved person. This is true because evolved individuals live to connect with others. Empathy comes easy, and they are usually super lovable characters. They love to love, and they love to be loved. Without insulting the evolved person, they are a little like Labrador retrievers. . . . loyal, heartfelt, loving, endearing, and selfless. Yet, when they have partners who withhold love, blame them for most things, and say and do insensitive things, the emotionally available person suffers. Again, without sounding insulting, it's like having a Labrador retriever and rarely petting and cuddling with it. The dog is going to blame itself and undoubtedly become depressed.

The unevolved person, because they are only capable of emotional distance—in addition to putting other people down and blaming other people because it makes them feel superior and good about themselves—do not suffer in the relationship. In fact, although they complain to their partner frequently about their partner's inadequacies, which is part of the cycle, they experience the relationship as fantastic—until the inevitable happens. The unavoidable thing I'm talking about is sex. When the emotionally evolved person feels emotional distance for too long, they sometimes lose their desire for physical intimacy, for obvious reasons. Deep and sensitive, they associate sex with a deep connection and love. So having sex without these feelings is often difficult for them. The unevolved person, on the other hand, feels entitled to sex whenever they want it and can be very demanding and harassing about it. The added guilt about avoiding sex can make an evolved person feel like they are the selfish and cold one in the relationship when the opposite is actually true.

Also, if they are neglected for too long, they start to long for love. Often, they invest everything in their children and work to sublimate for the cold and painful romantic relationship. Sometimes, they dive into hobbies or activities to fill the void. This infuriates their unevolved partner who does not like to see their partner happy with much of anything because they are very jealous.—Which, of course, adds to the hostility in the relationship.

CHAPTER 4

What to Do

S o, now that we have defined the emotionally evolved, emotionally unevolved, and articulated examples of what each looks like. . . . what to do if you are involved with an emotionally unevolved partner? The obvious answer is—think about ending the relationship. Yet, what if you are married to this person or have children with this person, or both? If this is the case, the answer is far more complicated and requires more evaluating.

The first thing that needs to be assessed is the extent of your partner's emotional arrest, and, the second is, do they pathologically project onto you? Let's grapple with the first concept. Your partner may be emotionally unevolved; however, they may be capable of learning the tools necessary to achieve emotional closeness in a relationship. In fact, because of our socialization tendencies in western culture, it's common for men to have little concrete knowledge about how to stay emotionally connected to their partner. Yet, if they were open to the idea and had a chance to experience and practice emotional closeness in a relationship, they might be able to grow and evolve. This open-mindedness is a great sign that they may be capable of emotional closeness. One quick way to test this is to discuss the shortcomings of your relationship and ask them to read this book. If they read the book, actually read the book, not just say they will, it is a very good sign. If the book resonates with them, and they can relate to the ideas, it is another green flag. Being open minded is a quality of the emotionally evolved. Also, their willingness to look at themselves, and reflect is another characteristic of the emotionally evolved. And, lastly, if they hold themselves accountable for some of their tendencies because of the book, STAY! Stay in the relationship. Your partner just needed some coaching. If counseling, therapy, or another book is a more effective medium, that's fantastic too.

The second important aspect in deciding if your partner is slightly unevolved or pathologically unevolved is figuring out if they pathologically project. Often, when a person is emotionally unevolved, they utilize a defense mechanism called projective identification. Unfortunately, when used to an extreme, projective identification is pathological and unhealthy. This is especially true for the partner of a projector because it is the partner that is the recipient of the negative projection, and they have little knowledge that they are being victimized because they are manipulated into blaming themselves. It's an insidious and unconscious defense mechanism, and it causes an enormous amount of damage.

In other words, neither partner is aware of the manipulation. The unevolved personality is unconsciously motivated by their own insecurities; flying on autopilot regarding their relations. They do not realize they are insecure because they immediately and unconsciously dump these insecurities into their partner. And because they instinctively deflect any personal accountability by turning things back on their partner and blaming them, they sincerely believe they are innocent of any wrongdoing, and they believe this so vehemently that they distort the facts in order to defend this belief. This distorted sense of reality is very dangerous because it does not correspond with what actually occurred. Because of this altered sense of reality, the unevolved person and evolved person battle about what transpired and often the evolved personality starts to doubt themselves and their sense of reality. Also, an unevolved person will minimize their actions in order to excuse them as well, claiming their partner is oversensitive and that what transpired was blown out of proportion.

A projector is someone who is emotionally unevolved, so they have a very fragile ego. Profoundly insecure, they compensate with narcissism, vanity, and an inflated sense of self-importance. Because their sense of self is so fragile and vulnerable, they use the defense mechanism, projective identification, to help themselves feel more secure. Unable to tolerate their negative qualities, they project them onto someone else. Then they see these qualities in that person and feel entitled to control, dominate, and reprimand that person. Because the concept is complicated, let's break it down. The first step in the process is projection.

One clear example of the psychological defense mechanism, projection, occurred with a teenage client of mine. Gifted academically, successful in several extracurricular activities, and extraordinarily kind and compassionate, Eve was emotionally evolved. After a year and a half of dating her boyfriend, and careful deliberation, she decided to have sex. When her friend got wind of her decision, she saddled up next to Eve at Eve's locker and stated, "You better be careful. You are going to end up pregnant and alone after a one night stand because he will leave you after you have sex!" Eve was stunned and speechless. She didn't know how to respond, and her friend flounced off after spouting off her statement. Although Eve was able to shake off the comment and move on with her day, it stung. Eve second guessed her decision and her boyfriend's loyalty. When she brought the situation to the session, she described the

---

Signs that your partner is a pathological projector include:

1. They regularly make sarcastic comments.
2. They frequently put down your ideas, opinions, or interests.
3. They speak to you in a commanding and demanding manner.
4. They lack empathy for you.
5. They believe they are right most, if not all of the time.
6. They believe things should be done their way without question.
7. They play the victim and feign hardship because of you.
8. They refuse to participate in much of anything you like or want to do.
9. They dismiss you.
10. They degrade you and put you down in front of your children.
11. They have isolated you from original family and friends.
12. They call you names.
13. They have publicly humiliated you on several occasions.
14. They antagonize and harass you.
15. They refer to you as emotional, oversensitive, or insinuate you misinterpret or make up situations in your head.

---

comment as "no big deal," but was clearly affected by it. After talking about it, she was reassured, and her confidence in her relationship with her boyfriend was reinstated.

Three weeks later she attended the session and disclosed that her friend was pregnant from a "one night stand." Her friend had gotten intoxicated at the party and had sex with someone she barely knew. Eve was astounded at the clarity of her friend's earlier projection. Her friend was terribly insecure and jealous of Eve, so she projected her own insecurities onto Eve to make Eve feel insecure, and herself feel better. Eve was able to remain in the friendship and supported her friend, but realized that her friend's stinging and degrading comments were really about how she felt about herself and not Eve.

Another example utilizing Eve and her friend occurred in Chemistry class. Eve was called out of class due to her involvement in a special school event. As she left class, her friend called out to her, "If you are going to leave early, you better be prepared to get a C on the exam!" Again, Eve was able to shrug the comment off, but the sting lingered. Her head swam with insecurities during the special event, and she had a difficult time enjoying herself. When the exams were returned, it was Eve's friend who received a C. Eve earned an A.

Because the friendship between Eve and her friend is not a close friendship, but rather a casual friendship, the projection affects Eve's self-esteem, but temporarily and without long term damage. In a romantic partnership, continuous toxic projections, are just that—toxic. They leave the recipient of the projection insecure, ashamed, and full of self-doubt. This is the identification aspect of the defense mechanism. Without realizing it, the recipient embodies the insecurities transferred to them by the projector. So much so, that they feel incompetent and worthless. Often, they believe they are lucky to have the projector in their lives because they don't think they are capable of making it on their own. Moreover, they feel that they sometimes deserve the mistreatment and excuse it because they are busy blaming themselves. This defense mechanism does not discriminate and can imprison educated, intelligent and successful individuals as easily as anyone else. Even psychotherapists can be tricked. It's elusive, insidious, and intangible.

Although projection is a universal defense mechanism, the difference between a normal projection and a pathological projection is the negativity of the material being projected and the need for the projector to project in order to feel secure and to maintain their psychological balance. This means that pathological projections are a characterological defense mechanism deeply rooted in the projector's psyche. Dangerous because of the projection strips the recipient of their self-esteem and identity, the relationship becomes detrimental to the emotionally evolved partner.

In summary, if your partner is mildly emotionally unevolved and simply lacks awareness about how to sustain emotional closeness in the relationship, there is hope. Yet, they have to be able to admit this and invest in the process of learning how. If your partner is severely emotionally unevolved, and they use projective identification, it is important to consider ending the relationship.

Yet, what if you have kids? A myth common in this culture is that staying together for the children is better for the children. This could not be further from the truth. Having a parent who is emotionally unevolved is painful for a child. The child doesn't receive empathy from this parent, and they are usually either blamed for everything that goes wrong or they are idealized and spoiled. Neither of these experiences is remotely healthy for a child. Also, the emotionally unevolved parent is often controlling, demanding, and critical, which is extremely disheartening, painful, and anxiety inducing for the child. They are frequently left alone with their worries because the emotionally unevolved parent is so consumed with how they feel; they are incapable of understanding how their child feels.

In addition, the emotionally unevolved parent uses the child to stroke their own ego. If the child makes them look good, they approve of the child. If the child does things that make the unevolved parent look less favorable, the unevolved parent will condemn and emotionally abandon the child. This is also a very destructive and abusive way to parent.

One last problematic dynamic occurring when a parent is emotionally unevolved is they are, by nature, very jealous. Mild jealousy is normal and universal, but an emotionally unevolved person is intensely and maliciously jealous. Their envy of other people runs so deep and is so intense that it motivates them to sabotage the person they are jealous of. This is a problem when their co- parent is an evolved person who probably is deeply connected to their children and enjoys the children immensely. Of course, the unevolved parent is continually jealous of the evolved parent's relationship with their children and attempts to undermine and sabotage it. Behind the evolved parent's back, the unevolved parent talks negatively about them to the children, often distorting the truth and telling untrue stories about the evolved parent. Frequently, the unevolved parent attempts to align the children with them and against the evolved parent. Often the unevolved parent acts like they are the evolved parent's boss, taking a superior and dominant role with their partner when the children are present. And, last, but not least, the unevolved parent always frames himself as the good guy and the evolved parent as the bad guy. Of course, occasionally he reinforces the evolved parent in order to have situations to refer to if the evolved parent ever dares bring it up.

These tactics become extreme during a breakup or divorce, and the evolved parent should never trust that the unevolved parent has the children's best interest at heart. This is because the unevolved parent is self-centered and egotistical. They don't have the capacity to put their children's welfare before their own, and, usually, are not the party that asked for the divorce. They become extremely enraged and very vindictive, aiming to destroy their partner and their partner's relationship with their children. This is exceptionally unhealthy for the children, so the evolved parent must not surrender to shared custody or more visitation. The evolved person must fight to be the primary caregiver in their children's lives because they are the healthiest and the children will be well-adjusted with them. In addition, the evolved parent must be honest with their children and find a way to enlighten the children about this dynamic without talking negatively about their parent.

Of course, the emotionally unevolved parent also attempts to assassinate the evolved parent's reputation with the outside world, as well. They will distort the truth and spread lies about the evolved parent to all of their mutual friends and the attorneys and judges involved, accusing the evolved parent of being an unfit parent. Although it is a nightmare, the evolved parent must not give up. They have to maintain their composure/dignity and let the unevolved parent's antics backfire.

An important thing to remember when separating or dissolving a relationship with an unevolved person is that they will attempt to reel you back into the relationship by acting nice. Manipulative and often charming, they will play nice for a while. When this occurs, it is difficult for the evolved person to stick to their guns. They frequently question their judgment when this happens. It is not uncommon for the evolved person, because of their forgiving and loyal nature, to give the unevolved person multiple chances, only to be hurt and mistreated again and again.

CHAPTER 5

Empathy as a Lost Art

So, if empathy is the answer to finding love and peace in most relationships, if it transforms the world for the good, allows us to transcend our physical limits, and is the answer to raising a happy and emotionally healthy children, why don't we do it? The question is perplexing, especially when professionals, whose job it is to be empathic, are not.

Empathy is why therapy works. Yet, many therapists like to be the expert, give advice, support, and help their client problem solve—but that does not heal their patient. That does not get their patient better. Can it improve their circumstance in many situations? Sure, but will it produce a long lasting positive change in their client's life? No. Empathy should always preempt advice, problem solving, and recommendations.

Empathy is the key to trust, respect, and closeness in every relationship. It is as rare as a yellow diamond. Sympathy, empathies corrupt sister, is what we are coaching our kids to have. This is counterproductive and leads to selfish and self-serving acts, as described previously. If people empathize with characters in novels, in the movies, and on TV, why is it largely absent from our everyday life? Why is the most important ingredient in our lives missing, and more importantly, why is it missing from our MOST precious and significant relationships?

There are several probable answers to this question.

1) Because individuals with personality disorders lack the capacity for empathy, and unfortunately, there are many undiagnosed personality disordered people.
2) People don't know how.
3) People are too absorbed with their own feelings to think about how someone else feels.
4) People are prone to telling other people what to do because this makes them feel powerful, but advice giving is a relatively selfish act if feelings are not empathized with first. It disempowers the injured party further. Collaborative problem solving and advice that is elicited are most effectively received after empathizing with the person's feelings.

The discussion about how to have empathy for another is imperative. It requires three steps. The first step in empathizing with someone is consciously making a mental shift. That is, a change from what you feel and think about the situation to thoughts about how the other person feels. This mental shift is the toughest step. Once the shift has been made and you have consciously set aside your own feelings and thoughts about the situation to try to understand the other person's, you are more than half way there. The second step is identifying and validating how your partner feels, and the third step is partnering with them on talking about what to do next.

Because the first step is the toughest, an example involving this step helps. Say your partner comes home distraught about a conflict with his boss, who is a bit of a bully. Of course, your first instinct is to tell your husband that his boss is wrong for multiple reasons and that your husband should send his boss an email saying. . . . , or tell the boss this. . . . , or meet with HR, or talk a colleague, or a dozen other solutions to his problems. That does not seem to help him feel better. In fact, it probably makes him feel worse and causes conflict between the two of you.

A more successful way to go about helping your partner is first to set aside your own thoughts and feelings about the situation. Then, think critically about how your partner feels. Does he feel hurt that his boss overlooked him for a responsibility? Does he feel incompetent because he made a mistake? Is he disappointed his boss did not follow through with what was promised? Identify your partner's feeling. "You are disappointed you didn't get the promotion. You have every right to be. I would be too if it were me."

This step gets tougher, however, when the conflict is within the relationship. For example, Anne was hurt that her husband and daughter glossed over her birthday without giving her a gift. They made dinner for her, but she was upset that they didn't put forth more of an effort. When she confessed her feelings to her husband the next day, he had several reasons for his lack of effort. This included that Anne had been in the hospital the week prior, and he felt the family was still recovering. He wasn't sure if she was up to going out to dinner, so he didn't make a reservation. And her youngest daughter was visiting the following week, so he thought a nice dinner with presents would be more meaningful then. Unfortunately, none of these reasons or excuses helped Anne feel better about the situation and they intensified her anger. Anne and her husband avoided each other for several days to avoid arguing about it.

A more effective way to handle the situation would be to have empathy for the hurt party, by identifying and validating their feelings. So, a better response would be, "You are really hurt. (Pause.) You feel like we don't care about you. I'm so sorry. I never intended to hurt your feelings.

Let's go to dinner tonight." It's essential to keep in mind that empathy only works when it is sincere, gentle, and delivered with a soothing tone, soft eye contact, and in best case scenarios, a hug.

Identifying your partner's feelings may seem confusing, but really it is not. There is a small list of feelings to choose from when your partner is upset:

What is Your Partner Feeling?	
1) Anger	8) Unloved
2) Hurt	9) Unappreciated
3) Disappointment	10) Insignificant
4) Betrayed	11) Overwhelmed
5) Ashamed	12) Frustrated
6) Embarrassed	13) Worried
7) Sad	14) Powerless

Again, authenticity and a gentle tone are imperative when attempting to identify how your partner feels. Eye contact and close physical proximity are also critical. If you are insincere, the attempt at empathy will feel patronizing to your partner. You have to speak from the heart.

An important aspect to keep in mind about anger is that anger is intense hurt. When an individual feels deep emotional pain, they often defend against the intensity of this hurt to protect themselves. Anger is, sometimes, the quickest defense. Often, this is the most common defense for men because they are frequently discouraged from showing vulnerability or shedding tears. Therefore, when your partner gets extremely angry at you, it's probable that you have actually hurt their feelings profoundly in some way. It's essential at this time to identify their anger and hurt and validate it. "You're so mad at me and very hurt. I understand." The difficulty, however, lies with the reality that when someone gets angry with you, you feel forced to leap to your own defense. Don't. Remember that anger is actually hurt. Arguing, defending your actions, and providing reasons for your behaviors intensifies the conflict and reignites hurt feelings. Empathize with the feelings fully, and then explain why you did what you did, and apologize.

Another point is that your partner might not even know themselves how they are feeling. They just know they are hurt and upset. It's absolutely ok to acknowledge this. This statement alone is empathic. "You are really upset." "You are so hurt." These statements, when delivered with care and genuine compassion is sometimes all the empathy your partner needs. Empathy is THAT powerful and transforming.

It is also important to mention that having empathy for your partner doesn't always mean admitting fault. One partner can have empathy for their partner without taking responsibility for the situation when they are sincerely innocent. For example, let's say Bob is approached by his ex-girlfriend while at dinner with Julie. Julie is in the restroom when Bob's ex approaches him and sits down next to him. When Julie returns, Bob's ex is only half way through a long story she is determined to finish. Julie sits across the table, furious at the interruption and at Bob. Her food is getting colder, and her mood is getting darker. Finally, the ex finishes her monolog, hugs Bob, and flounces off.

Bob's initial response is critical at this moment. The nice peaceful dinner can be salvaged or it will go down in flames. What does Bob say? These are some choices:

A) "You are mad, and you have every right to be. I'm furious too."
B) "I didn't do anything. She just sat down and started talking. You were in the restroom too long."

C) "I guess you're pretty disappointed. We have been planning this dinner for months. I bet you feel a little betrayed, too. I totally understand. I would feel the same way. I wish she would have stopped talking for a second so I could have asked her to leave."

D) "Clearly she's not over me. I think she wants to get back together with me."

Hopefully, the responses A and C sound empathic. The feelings anger, hurt, disappointment, and betrayal, are identified and validated. And, although, Bob empathizes with Julie's feelings, he doesn't admit fault—because he was not at fault. He does empathize with how Julie felt in the situation which is necessary. An essential point to note is that if someone immediately states a litany of excuses for a situation, and acts defensive, they seem guilty. Anytime an individual makes excuses, and launches a "But, I didn't do anything wrong" campaign, this readily emits guilt. Therefore, having confidence and security in yourself to set your own thoughts and feelings aside for a moment, to have empathy for someone else, is the evolved thing to do, and it will preserve the awesomeness of your relationship.

Moreover, an empathic statement only takes a few minutes. Although it requires a mental and emotional shift on the empathizer's behalf because it is a selfless emotional act which requires energy, it only takes a few seconds to verbalize. Countering someone's hurt feelings with reasons and explanations is equivalent to telling them they shouldn't have hurt feelings, which is not acceptable. Telling someone their feelings are invalid causes further distress and the continuation of conflict will zap time, energy, fun, and peace for hours and sometimes days.

Let's use Ben and his girlfriend as an example. They decided to play a friendly game of tennis, yet when Ben's girlfriend won the set, Ben angrily hit a tennis ball across the park immediately after losing a tennis match to his girlfriend, yet denied it was an angry act and excused it by saying the tennis ball was bad, and he needed to get rid of it. However, the timing of the incident and the anger he had emitted after losing the match made his argument less believable. Also, he attempted to make his girlfriend feel crazy for even "thinking such a thing," and that "she was crazy." The conflict intensified and feelings of trust and closeness were not resumed.

Now, if he was genuinely innocent and was not acting out of anger, but was only getting rid of a bad ball, all he had to do was empathize with his girlfriend's feelings and the fight would be over. For example, saying, "I understand why you are upset. It looked like I was throwing a fit. I would have thought the same thing if I were you." Following those statements, throwing his arm around her and complimenting her tennis would probably end the fight, and they would go on with the rest of their Saturday happy.

If he was guilty, and he cranked the ball across the park because he was acting like a sore loser, all that was necessary was to take responsibility for the immature act and empathize with his girlfriend's feelings. "That was so juvenile. I'm sorry. My masculine pride got the best of me. I bet it shocked and upset you. I'm sorry."

Using this example, we can move on to step number three, partnering with the injured party and asking what can be done to help them feel better about the situation. For example, after he empathized with his girlfriend's feelings and held himself accountable (if he needed to), saying something like, "What would make you feel better about this?" In most situations the empathy and accountability are more than enough. But, if she's as smart as she is good at tennis, she'll say "a back rub."

Other suggestions include, "What can I do to help?" "Can I try and take your mind off of it?" "Ice cream?" "Wine?" "Dirty joke?" But, remember, steps 1 and 2 are necessary before three. Hopefully, step three includes something fun. Also, it is not surprising if step 3 leads to physical intimacy because empathy is one of the sexiest gifts a person can get from their partner. Experiencing empathy from your partner reestablishes and solidifies emotional closeness, which often transforms into physical intimacy.

In the case of Bob and Julie, step 3 would include, "How can I make this up to you, honey?" "What would help you feel better?" "What can I do to help?" A thoughtful gesture is also effective. So, using the example of Bob and Julie, maybe since dinner was tarnished, Bob suggests they go to Julie's favorite café where they can share a pastry for dessert.

In a world where practicality reigns, protect your romantic union from it. There is not a more significant investment in the world than your relationship with your romantic partner or your children, so spend thought, time, and money on these relationships because it will save you gallons of stress and sadness in the end. Don't be extravagant with your material possessions. Be lavish with how you love. Make spontaneity, fun, and adventure a constant in these relationships. They are your most important endeavors in life, by far.

Although these examples have utilized women as the upset party in the relationship, men are as much in need of empathy and emotional closeness in their relationships as women are. The concepts apply to both genders. It might look a touch different with a man, but not much. Let's use the example of Gabby and Ron. Ron texted Gabby and asked Gabby if she would pick up his son, Jack, who was at a friend's house in the same neighborhood, and take him to his job on the way home from book club, since it was on her route home. Ron was across town and caught in traffic. This required that Gabby leave book club fifteen minutes ahead of schedule, and Gabby did not want to leave her book club early. She stalled in her response to Ron and texted him that she was annoyed at his request. Finally, at the last minute, she texted Ron and said she would do it.

When she got home that night, Ron was quiet. Gabby knew she had been selfish for not agreeing immediately, and for giving Ron grief about his request. What should Gabby's response be?

A) The only "me" time I have during the month is book club. You should have planned for traffic. It's your fault.

B) He, technically, is not my kid, so I shouldn't have to sacrifice something important for your mistake.

C) I bet you were so hurt when I said "no," initially. You had every right to be. I was selfish for a few minutes there. I'm sorry. What can I do to make it up to you?

D) I can't imagine how you felt when I didn't respond. You were probably feeling powerless to help your son who needed to get to work on time, and you thought you could count on me in a pinch. I let you down for a minute there. I'm sorry.

The empathic response is either C or D. Instead of making excuses and only thinking about herself and her feelings, Gabby set them aside and thought about how Ron must have felt when he reached out to her for help and she was reluctant. Because she was able to set her own feelings aside for a moment to think about Ron's, she was able to be empathic.

In essence, nothing in your life is worth more than your romantic relationship or your children. When their importance is tested, prove your love. Do not let them down. The words "I love you" mean nothing unless you can back it up. Be selfless when you get the chance. It will feel wonderful.

In addition, children are around for a short period of time before they are off on their own. The few years between your child walking and driving, pass like the blink of an eye. So, enjoy, invest, stay attuned and empathize. It seems parents are focused on their child achieving and behaving, which are important things to focus on, but staying attuned to their emotional state, helping them with their worries, and empathizing with them is a parent's most important job. Yet, it is lost on us most of the time. So, if parents understood one important fact, it might help. All behavior, the good, the bad, and the ugly, is driven by feelings. If you understand the feelings, you can change behavior immediately, and indefinitely.

It only takes a few seconds, but it will deepen your relationship with your child and create emotional health. Let's take Ben for an example. Ben hated Mondays. It was his mom's long and late day at work. One morning, he whined and cried about how much he "hated" Mondays. Instead of spending time reiterating the necessity of working long and late on Mondays, and why school was necessary and important for Ben, she naturally empathized with his feelings. She stated, "I know, honey. I hate Mondays too. My stomach has the same pit in it as yours, because I miss you when I'm at work, just like you miss me when you are at school." With that, Ben came to her for a hug and didn't complain again. He got ready for school and plunged into his day with determination. A little empathy goes a long way, and it's the one intervention that dissipates a child's anxiety on the spot.

A second example involves Ben, as well. One day Ben came home and realized his sister had beat him back to the house and had taken apart one of the toys he had built. Furious, he screamed, "I hate you, Mary," and he threw his backpack across the laundry room. Now, most parents would agree that this is an ugly display. The behaviors are inappropriate and should be addressed, but the feeling is understandable.

So, instead of sending Ben to his room because of the fit of anger, a parent should take a few seconds to show some empathy first. "You are really mad. You have every right to be. I would be too—but you cannot be mean. Please apologize to your sister and pick up your backpack." Contrary to popular opinion, anger is a human emotion and it is normal. What a person does with their anger is the issue. Because Ben's was empathized with, his anger turned into frustration, and he told his mom he had invited a friend over that day to play with the very toy his sister disassembled. His mom continued to empathize with his frustration and told Ben after he apologized and picked up his backpack, she would help him reassemble the toy.

Parents have a difficult time tolerating their child's anger because it is never a pleasant display. Yet it is THE most important emotion to learn how to regulate appropriately; so helping a child digest anger is critical. Again, a few empathic words can help a child metabolize any negative feeling rather quickly. If Ben's mom had been upset by his angry fit and immediately sent him to his room to "calm down," Ben is left with no help regulating his anger. In fact, if she sends him to his room she is actually instructing him to stifle his anger because it is a shameful emotion. Unfortunately, we all know what happens to individuals who stifle their anger. It leads to dangerous explosions. Individuals who regulate their anger are usually emotionally intelligent.

Parenting is not about teaching your child right from wrong; it is about showing them empathy, compassion, love, and guidance. If you are not attuned to your child's worries, insecurities, and fears, you are not doing enough as a parent. Providing children with what they need and sometimes what they want is only one tenth of the parenting job. The rest is about emotional closeness. Empathy is the first element of emotional closeness, but as established previously, personal accountability is the other critical component.

Again, some parents have a false notion that they must be right 100% of the time, or they lose their authority as a parent. This could not be further from reality. The only possible way for a child to learn personal accountability is by experiencing their parent holding themselves personally accountable within the relationship.

Let's take Matt and his mom, Rachel, as an example. One busy morning, Rachel was trying to get everyone to school and work on time. She told her first grade son, "Matt, go get your socks and shoes on." As she was in the kitchen grabbing lunches, Matt approached her giggling with a muffin in his mouth and looked down at the floor. Rachel, who thought Matt was clowning around and purposefully spilling muffin crumbles on the floor, yelled at Matt. Matt, stunned and hurt, burst into tears and ran to the garage door. On his way, he cried, "I hate you!" Shocked and confused at what had transpired, Rachel realized that he had his socks and shoes on as he was running to the door. She had made a mistake. She thought Matt was clowning around and purposefully making a mess, when he was really just eating his muffin and looking down in an attempt to proudly show her that he had put his socks and shoes on. She realized she had made a serious mistake. As difficult as it was, Rachel gave up on the mission to be on time that morning and she went out into the garage, crawled in the back seat of the car, looked her son in the eye, and said, "I made a big mistake. I'm sorry. I hurt you. You were trying to show me that you had done what I asked and I didn't understand and I yelled at you. I was wrong. I am sorry. I love you." With that, Matt crawled close to her and said, "It's ok momma." Rachel could have yelled at Matt for saying, "I hate you!" But she realized she had made the mistake. She took responsibility for it and apologized. She repaired the rift and restored the emotional closeness.

As parents, we are troubled by bad behavior, but what we don't realize sometimes is that our children learn most of their behaviors from us, and if we look at ourselves honestly, we actually might be the catalyst. Because Lucy is a parent who is self-reflective and insightful, she was able to hold herself accountable for her relationship with her son. This moment brought her and her son together, emotionally, and facilitated trust and love. There are times when a power struggle is inevitable, and the parent needs to win, but most of the time, empathy and accountability will do the trick and do it quickly. Moreover, empathy and accountability in no way mean a parent is backing down or surrendering to a bad behavior. They are simply acknowledging the feelings first. A brief, succinct statement which empathizes with the child's feelings while still holding them accountable for negative behaviors is effective. Some examples include, "Ben, it is ok to be mad, but it is not ok to hit." "Molly, it is ok to be angry, but it is not ok to say mean things." "Melanie, I know you are frustrated, but you cannot throw your coat on the floor."

So, when are power struggles necessary? Power struggles are crucial when a child's safety or well-being is at risk. Parents must make their kids go to school. They must make their children bathe and brush their teeth. Eating healthy is also a necessity, along with doing homework and going to bed on time. Kids should not be allowed to do unsafe things with friends. So, if a power struggle is necessary, how can you make it as least painful as possible?

Three useful tips to implement when you find yourself locking horns with your child include; reverse psychology, giving your child choices, and reframing. Reverse psychology is the most fun. If you want your child to eat her broccoli before leaving the dinner table, dare her not to. Beg her not to. Say things like, "Don't eat that broccoli on your plate. Don't do it! Don't you dare?" This perplexes your child for a moment and then usually makes them giggle. The more emphatic you can be, the more fun and effective the tool is. So, once your child smiles and picks up a stalk, keep at it. "Don't put that in your mouth. Don't do it. Don't you dare?" Kids love to feel like they are in control, and reverse psychology sets them up to be. It also gets everybody laughing which alleviates tension and makes everybody more agreeable.

The second trick is to give your child choices. So, if demanding they do something is not working, give them a choice. For example, if you tell them to sit down, and they refuse, say, "You can sit on this bench or this chair, your choice." Other examples include, "Do you want to put your bike away in the garage or at the top of the driveway?" "Do you want peas or carrots for dinner?" Instead of commanding or demanding, you are empowering them to do what you need them to do, AND they feel in control in a healthy way.

The third technique for turning a power struggle into a cooperative interaction is reframing. So, when tension is building, and a power struggle is about to ensue, call your child's attention to something else around you that is funny or entertaining. Breaking the tension and changing the mood helps downplay a power struggle. Then, when returning to the task at hand, change the parameters up to make it seem less dreadful to the child. For example, if a child does not want to go to the restroom before getting into the car to embark on a long road trip, say, "ok, if we don't go to the bathroom now, we might have to stop and pee-pee at the side of the road or go poop in a poopy port-o-potty. I'm going to go too. Whoever's done first wins!" A side tip: anything with the words poo and pee in it will make them laugh between the ages of two and eight—sad, but true. A couple of minutes is all that is necessary to get your child out of their stubborn mood and into a more agreeable one.

In essence, cooperation, empathy and accountability not only allow a parent to stay close with their child, but it produces a happy, healthy, well- adjusted human being, which should be the goal. A child with a secure sense of self means they won't bully, lie, cheat, or steal. It also means they will have empathy and compassion for others and a strong work ethic. A child with their own internal moral compass doesn't need to be taught right from wrong; they feel it in their heart. They have character.

So, if empathy dissipates a child's worries, and emotional closeness with a parent produces a child who is if free from anxiety and depression, it is safe to conclude that adults are far less anxious and depressed when they have an emotionally close partnership. This seems like common sense, but millions of Americans take medicine to treat their anxiety and depression instead of evaluating the health of their relationship. Also, divorce is often designated the easy way out, and people are often advised to stay in their marriage for the kids. Yet an unhealthy union is terrible for the entire family's mental health. Thus, therapy, counseling, and a solid understanding of what emotional closeness is and how to sustain it in your relationship are imperative. If emotional closeness cannot be achieved, divorce is the bravest and healthiest choice for everyone involved.

In addition, if a couple is working on emotional closeness, it is important that they are not defensive. Empathy is almost impossible to provide if you are defensive and anxious. One important way to reduce defensiveness and anxiety, outside of counseling, is to practice connecting the mind and the body. Reestablishing and sustaining the mind and body connection, soothes, focuses, and grounds human beings. Although an Eastern philosophy, the mind and body connection is becoming more popular in Western cultures. Traditional practices include yoga, martial arts, tai chi, acupuncture, massage therapy, and meditation.

There are many activities which connect the mind and the body. Essentially any physical activity that requires focused concentration to perform is a mind and body activity. Dance is an example. Sports are also examples. When the mind and the body are unified, the individual feels whole and alive. If these activities are performed regularly, the mind body connection is sustained for longer periods of time. When a person feels whole and alive, they do not feel defensive or anxious. In addition, the mind and body connection allow a person to be "mindful." Mindfulness is defined as the intentional accepting and non-judgmental focus of one's attentions on the emotions, thoughts and sensations occurring in the present moment, which can be trained by meditational practices. Essentially, mindfulness allows for self- reflection, self-actualization, emotional regulation, and empathy. It is an effective practice to engage in, not only to reduce anxiety and stress but to prime individuals for emotional closeness.

CHAPTER 6

The Unevolved Couple

Unevolved + Unevolved = Happiness

Although an emotionally evolved person and an emotionally unevolved person feel discontent because of the mismatch in emotional availability, an unevolved person and another unevolved person sometimes work. Why? An unevolved person is not interested in emotional closeness. They are, however, keenly interested in being superficially gratified. Essentially, superficial gratification is all they really care about. In most cases it is either money, power, and/or sex that they find gratifying. For example, a wealthy man might want a beautiful woman to have on his arm and to satisfy him sexually. A beautiful woman might want a wealthy man, so she can have the material things she needs in order to have status and power in her social circle. A career minded woman might want a husband who will stay home with the kids and do all of the domestic duties, so she can sustain her powerful position at work, which gratifies her need for power. The unevolved couple is content as long as their partner is gratifying them with either money, sex, status, or power. It is a business deal. Emotional closeness, empathy, accountability, and shared joy, are not necessary for them. They are content as long as their partner fulfills their assigned role. As superficial as a business deal, it works because the unevolved couple is predominately shallow. Of course, they do not see themselves as such, but it is obvious. They perceive themselves as deep people because they love the things that gratify them, whether it's their partner or kids. However, this love evaporates when their kids stop gratifying them, or their partner stops gratifying them, which qualifies their love as conditional and superficial. They love people as if they are possessions instead of human beings.

Unfortunately, although this arrangement works, neither are extremely happy, and both are fixated with the superficial. Because of this obsession, they need more and more money, status, or sex to feel gratified. Unable to take responsibility for their own unhappiness, they need to be satisfied through superficial means, and if this doesn't happen, they retaliate. They blame their partner for their own unhappiness and often cheat or spend recklessly. Believing they are justified, because their partner is not giving them what they want, they feel entitled to buy whatever they want or have sex with who ever they want. Yet, if they sustain their roles and continue to increasingly gratify their partner's increasing needs, the union works. Often, they objectify each other. They treat each other as sex objects or a money making machine and they only value their partner for these things. Frequently, they complain and denigrate their partner to others behind their partner's back.

However, if they can continue to get their needs met, meaning they can develop another business deal—for example if one partner agrees to look the other way while their partner cheats if he can continue to provide financially for her, the partnership will work. Because they are both superficial and vain, gratifying another superficially is all that it takes.

The reason this doesn't occur with an evolved and unevolved partnership is because one partner longs for emotional closeness and needs this emotional closeness as most red-blooded, feeling, human beings do.

And, they need kindness and empathy. They need to know they are valued and cherished as they cherish others. They are deep, and they live to love, deeply, selflessly, and sincerely. The emotionally unevolved belong together. Water meets its own level.

Moreover, an emotionally unevolved partner rarely wants to leave an emotionally evolved partner. Why? Because deep down they know they are out matched. The character and sensitivity of an evolved partner is fertile breeding ground for the unevolved partner to exploit. Like a black lab, the loyalty, humility, and sublimeness of a person with good character is perfect for the unevolved to use and abuse for their own good. Deep down the unevolved sense their partner's goodness and they want to get it. They want the essence of who their partner is, and the only way to get at it is through control and domination. They believe their partner is their possession, and they feel entitled to strip their partner's strong character and creative ideas from them and use it for their own benefit. All the while, the evolved person trusts and has faith that their partner has their best interest at heart when the opposite is actually true.

CHAPTER 7

The Evolved Couple

Happily Ever After

Two evolved people usually spend their lives happily ever after. Why? Because they are able to sustain emotional closeness. They are receptive to their partner's viewpoint which facilitates cooperation, compromise, and empathy. Also, their open mind and interest in the world motivates them to try the new things their partner is interested in. Because an evolved person is generally happy, they are often excited, upbeat, and usually embrace a good time. Also, because they feel fulfilled emotionally, they are less apt to spend, eat, or drink their loneliness away which saves them from a host of extraneous issues.

Because they have the capacity for empathy and personal accountability, they usually have similar styles regarding parenting and they reinforce each other when necessary. Their children not only benefit from their parent's empathy and accountability, but also their united front. Selfless in nature, the couple frequently sacrifices their personal needs for the family, knowing this investment is the most valuable of their lives. The workload is shared, and both people contribute equally to running the family and making decisions for the family. Good-natured teasing and a strong senses of humor keep the fun alive.

As it does for everyone when tragedy or trauma occurs, the couple supports each other. Their empathy for one another keeps them afloat, and their resilience and tenacity fuel their recovery. Thinking outside the box fosters creative problem solving, which is sometimes a very necessary skill with children. Although conflict and disagreement occur regularly, resolving the conflict and meeting each other half way is the norm with an evolved couple. Forgiveness and learning from mistakes are also common. Resentment and bitterness rarely exist for any lengthy period of time. However, if there is a time when these negative emotions linger it's during the first year they have a baby. The first year with a baby is tumultuous, overwhelming, exhausting, and riffled with change. The chances of the couple having difficulties during this time are strong. Yet, because it is temporary, the couple doesn't have a lot of trouble re-establishing their connection in the long run.

Let's use Anne and Mitch as an example. Tragically, they lost their two-year-old son to a brain aneurysm. This experience qualifies as the most excruciating of all human experiences. Neither Anne nor Mitch blamed the other, and both supported one another through their grief. When one person needed to talk about their feelings, the other listened empathically. They share in their son's memory regularly. A few years after their son passed away, they had another baby, and it is obvious, every day, that they cherish their daughter. Instead of allowing pain and grief to overcome their lives, they enjoy every moment with their daughter. Often, they use humor and good natured teasing to make each other laugh and to connect with each other, and their true priority is each other and their family. Essentially, an evolved couple can get through just about anything due to their empathy, compassion for one another, and personal accountability in the relationship.

CHAPTER 8
Dating

I f you are an evolved person and you are dating, watch out! The unevolved and the evolved are naturally attracted to each other, and as described already, this is not always a healthy or long lasting union. So, why is there chemistry between the unevolved and evolved? Because the evolved are painfully aware of their shortcomings and it's a relief sometimes to be around someone who doesn't feel they have any. The unevolved personality is fairly narcissistic and vain, yet this looks like confidence initially. The unevolved person seems larger than life in some respects. The evolved person, on the other hand, is humble and self-effacing. Self-critical and evaluating, so they are amazed at the unevolved person's ability to care less what other people think. Yet, this is not because the unevolved partner is genuinely confident. It is because they believe they are better than most people.

Also, the unevolved personality is manipulative, so they take great strides to make a good impression in front of the evolved person initially. Their real nature rears its ugly head the minute they believe they have their partner reeled in. Often during the wooing process, the unevolved personality slowly and subtly isolates the evolved person from their support system, and during their relationship, the unevolved personality often takes over the responsibility for many of the resources, most specifically, the financial resources. This arouses a feeling of dependence on the evolved person because they have not hung on to many resources of their own.

Also, the unevolved person talks a big game during the dating process but then changes their mind once they have the evolved person dependent on them. For example, the unevolved person may say they want children, but when they are married they may abandon this agreement. Also, present while dating, is the unevolved person's calculated displays of sympathy in order to convince the evolved person that they have a "good heart." Similarly, the unevolved person sprinkles niceties on the evolved person in the midst of their attempts to control and dominate their partner to camouflage their manipulations. These tactics are confusing for the evolved person who is fundamentally trusting, forgiving, and appreciative of friendly gestures.

One way for an evolved person to assess whether their partner is unevolved while dating is to give their partner the empathy test. Again, it is easy for an unevolved person to provide sympathy and support, but it is unlikely they can take responsibility for themselves within the romantic partnership, so test it. Go to them and gently explain that they hurt your feelings about something. See how they respond. If they are able to understand how you feel and apologize for hurting your feelings, whether they meant to or not, great. If they continually argue with you about why your feelings are wrong and you should not be hurt, you might need to continue to evaluate the healthiness of the relationship. A person who continually accuses you of being emotional, irrational, oversensitive or crazy when you bring an issue to them, is, most likely emotionally unevolved.

Let's revisit the example of Ben and his girlfriend, Julie. They both enjoyed tennis, but Julie had been having trouble with her forehand. Frustrated for most of the match, she struggled to win some points. However, before the last few games, she started to work out her forehand issue and won several games. The match became close, and Ben called several of Julie's balls out when Julie saw they were in. Annoyed, but happy her forehand was back to normal, she continued to play hard and won the match. Ben, who appeared angry, walked over to the bench picked up a tennis ball that had rolled under the bench and ferociously smacked it over the fence and into the field behind the courts. Julie was shocked. It appeared to Julie that Ben was so angry he lost to her that he had a temper tantrum and cracked a ball across the park out of anger.

Julie confronted Ben and asked him why he did it. Ben hemmed and hawed and said the ball was bad, and he wanted to get rid of it. This just didn't seem right to Julie. Why would he immediately crack a ball angrily over the fence after losing the match if he wasn't throwing a fit because she beat him? But, Ben refused to admit it. He made it seem like Julie was crazy for thinking this and accused her of picking a fight. Adamant that he had hit the ball out of anger that he had lost to her, she walked across the tennis courts and field and found the tennis ball. It was a new ball. She walked back to Ben and handed it to him. Ben still refused to take responsibility for his immature and ugly display of anger. Julie's anger increased because Ben refused to take responsibility for his behavior and blamed her for "imagining" things and causing conflict.

This seems like a small incident, but the serious problem with this scenario is Ben's refusal to take responsibility for his actions within the relationship. Julie experienced several more situations where Ben refused to admit fault or take responsibility for his behaviors while simultaneously turning the situation around in order to blame Julie. Of course, when this angered Julie, Ben referenced her anger and called her "out of control." The rift caused by these experiences are serious because conflict is rarely resolved, and trust and is not restored. In addition, the Julie in the relationship is left angry and hurt quite a bit while the Ben in the relationship, excuses himself from any wrongdoing and moves on happily. Emotional closeness is lost, and emotional distance grows with every passing day.

CHAPTER 9

Men and the Unfair Stereotype and Empathy as a Super Power

Unfortunately, our culture has excused emotionally unevolved tendencies, such as a refusal to take responsibility in a relationship, admit fault, or understand someone else's viewpoint, as masculine tendencies. This is extremely unfair and detrimental to everyone. It's akin to the metaphor, "men don't ask directions." This metaphor is outdated since the advent of GPS and maps on our phones, but it conveys a cultural stereotype. The belief that men are from Mars and women are from Venus, furthers the confusion and stereotypes about men, which are not accurate. Are men different from women? Yes. Absolutely. But, does this mean they are incapable of emotional closeness? Not the evolved men. Emotional closeness equates to love and happiness for both genders and all children. Emotional closeness is synonymous with healthy satisfying relationships, and in children, a strong sense of self.

In society today, referring to a man as sensitive or emotional is similar to calling a woman big boned. In a man, sensitivity and emotion insinuate weakness or a lack of masculinity. Yet, it is the emotionally evolved men who are the bravest and toughest. Take, for example, Louis

Zamperini, a man who transcended his own physical limits because of his empathy for others. He continually sacrificed his own needs and wishes to help his fellow soldiers. His empathy allowed him to surpass what was physically possible for a human being to save his friends from losing the last ounce of dignity that was allowing them to hold on to their lives. His empathy, which is comprised of sensitivity and emotion, made him more powerful (naked, starving, and diseased) than an entire country of armed soldiers. His empathy saved his friends' lives.

A few years ago, on the Lakefront of Lake Michigan, a man was swimming with his nephew and two nieces. His own children were younger and were on the beach building a sand castle. That day a wicked undertow swirled right around where his nephew and nieces were swimming and started to carry them out to the middle of the Lake Michigan. Realizing they were being swept away, they struggled against the current, panicked and exhausted, trying to get back to safety. Their uncle, realizing how strong the undertow was, and knowing the kids would soon be out of reach with no help, he called for help and then went after them, one by one. He swam as fast as he could and, one by one, he towed his family in. With the last breath he was able to muster, he swam the last child to the end of a pier where a bystander was able to grab the child and pull him to safety, and he went under. Gone. He gave his nieces and his nephew his last breath so they could live. He saved the lives of three children but had to give up his own to do it. That is empathy. That is a hero.

Martin Luther King, one of the bravest men to walk the face of this earth, who faced a force of hate every day and looked it straight in the eye without wavering, was one of the most evolved human beings who has existed. Continually sacrificing himself, to try and stop people from spreading hate, violence, humiliation, and degradation, he dedicated and sacrificed his life, so others could live without having their dignity stripped from them every day.

Abraham Lincoln is, yet, another example of a strong man who was emotionally evolved and capable of intense empathy. The emancipator of slaves, he used empathy to end slavery and unite a nation. Without the ability to feel for the plight of others, he would never have been able to make such an effective and successful humanitarian move. Another similar example is Gandhi, who led campaigns for easing poverty, expanding women's rights, building religious and ethnic amity and civil rights. Empathy is a powerful emotion. It can not only allow a person to transcend their own physical limitations, but it allows a human being the ability to transform the world with kindness and compassion.

Army reservist, Joe Darby, discovered horrendous abuses of prisoners by his buddies at Iraq's Abu Ghraib Prison in 2004. Although difficult to compromise his loyalty to friends, he exposed the terrible violence. His empathy and respect for human dignity and life ended violent atrocities. To highlight a point, any time a human being feels their life is more valuable than someone else's—just because they are a particular race, religion, or an American, or have money, or a higher degree, and then feels entitled to violate others because they believe they are higher on the "food chain",—they are no better than a terrorist like Osama Ben Laden who had the same belief, or the prison guards in the POW war camp in Japan. Violence begets violence. If you act violently and not in the name of self-defense, you are the same as a violent offender. If someone threatens your life, by all means, fight. If you are the attacker, and feel justified in your attack because you are "better than" another human being in your mind, you need to stop and get professional help.

All of the men listed above are some of the bravest men who have existed. They are also insatiable fighters. They fight with their mind, spirit, and heart. They fight tirelessly and selflessly for others. They are the exact opposite of weak and cowardly. Their capacity for empathy allows them to transcend their own physical limits. All of them sacrificed their life for others.

On the other hand, if you look at the world's greatest villains, several stereotypical masculine tendencies are apparent: power, control, and force. Their way is the right way, and any other idea is wrong. They violently punish any dissent. They attempt to control everyone through fear. They believe they are better than everyone else. Through propaganda and distortions of the truth, they align people with them and against their target. Some examples include Hitler, Mussolini, Ben Laden, and Stalin. Stealing another human being's dignity to oppress them is their most effective tool, believing they have the right to take someone's life because they are superior to them is common. Morally superior to others is how they perceive themselves, so murder, as they see it, is their right and their privilege.

So, why are we confusing pathological and maniacal tendencies as masculine? They are not. They are indicative of a weak self-esteem and a fragile identity which needs to be inflated with money or power to feel stable. These pathological tendencies are present in both females and males and need to be confronted despite the gender of the aggressor.

Thus, when encountering a powerful person as a potential romantic partner, attempt to distinguish whether they are confident or narcissistic? Do they treat people according to their place in a human hierarchy or do they value and respect others regardless of their financial or social status? Are they two different people around people they deem ordinary, and people they believe are more powerful? Ask them to visit a soup kitchen with you. Do they scoff and say, "Let's just write a check," or will they go? If you are dating a powerful woman or man who places great importance on their social status, invite them to visit a homeless shelter. Will they go?

Empathy is not a female or male tendency. It is a human tendency, and it is a superpower. Don't let anyone tell you different. Without empathy none of the heroes listed could have done what they did. Empathy is the fuel that allows people to do miraculous and brave acts. A strong sense of empathy enables you to know others and how they feel quickly. It bonds people to you and fosters closeness. But feeling sorry for someone, giving charity, or crying at TV commercials does not mean you have empathy. Empathy is the sincerest form of bravery, self-sacrifice, and love. It should not be confused with sympathy or charity, which are two self-serving behaviors.

Moreover, women are just as likely to be emotionally unevolved as men, but unfortunately, unevolved tendencies have largely been attributed to men. Separating the pathological tendencies of emotionally unevolved people from general male tendencies is critical. We want to marry heroes. We want to raise heroes. We want to be heroes.

Someone who demands obedience from their partner or their children, and feels entitled to have the final deliberation on decisions regarding their partner or their children, or they withhold resources, levy punishment, and sabotage them behind their backs, is like being in a relationship with a dictator. Power and control do not equate to love. An abused dog will eventually bite back or run away. But, if you love and cherish a dog they will be loyal until their last breath. The same is true for human beings. Respect the ones you love and you will be respected. Cherish and love empathically and you will be loved deeply in return.

A word of warning regarding empathy and the unevolved. Unfortunately, because empathy is a profound and complicated emotion. The unevolved are not only incapable of experiencing true empathy for someone else, but they also are incapable of accepting it, and often they will use it against the empathic person. Most of an unevolved person's emotion are superficial and relate to gratification. A lot of the time, this gratification comes in the form of money, power, or possessions. Unfortunately, this includes their children. Deriving pleasure from their children when their children make them look good is common. However, if the child veers from what the unevolved parent wants, they will frequently withhold their love, resources, and approval.

In the case of a divorce, an emotionally unevolved parent will unscrupulously put their children in the middle and often exploit the children against their partner in order to hurt their partner. They have little concern about what that does, psychologically to the child, but instead are gratified by the revenge they seek. Also, they often use the empathy against the evolved person.

Let's take, for example, Melissa and Eric. Eric, an evolved individual, filed for divorce from Melissa because he felt it was a cold and loveless marriage. Melissa dragged the divorce process out for years to spite Eric. Yet, Eric found another woman to spend time with who was warm and loving. Melissa, incensed that Eric was undeterred by the lengthy divorce process, in addition to his decision get involved with someone else, was enraged with anger and jealousy. She continually talked negatively about Eric, his new friend, repeatedly sharing her feelings with their children. She subjected them to very adult information and engaged in some unscrupulous behaviors. One night, she invited Eric to dinner to talk. She explained how hurt she was and blamed Eric. Eric felt terrible and apologized profusely. Then, she said that if she could have Eric's friend's ex-husbands information so she could talk to someone about how to cope with a divorce, she would be grateful. Of course, because Eric felt awful for hurting Melissa, he gave her the information.

In the next few weeks, Melissa proceeded to contact Eric's friend's ex-husband continually to gain personal information about Eric's friend which she maliciously distorted and broadcast to the community through social media. She also attempted to use the distorted information in court to try to prevent Eric's friend from having contact with their children. Fortunately, the judge was savvy enough to see through the manipulations and denied her request. This exemplifies how an unevolved person uses their partner's empathy against them.

Also, when an evolved individual is the target for an unevolved person, it is important for the evolved person to sustain their stance in spite of the unevolved person's bullying, threatening, and harassing. It is also typical for the evolved partner to disdain their unevolved partner because of their experience of being bullied, attacked, humiliated, maliciously harassed, and stripped of their dignity by their unevolved partner. Having intense dislike and anger towards another human being is uncomfortable for an evolved human being who has a good nature and wants to get along with everyone. Yet these negative feelings are inevitable when a human being is faced with someone attempting to destroy their self-esteem. Sometimes, the evolved partner feels guilty for disliking the unevolved individual, and they wonder why they cannot forgive. They cannot forgive until the unevolved person stops their attack. For example, if Loius Zamperini would have forgiven the guard while he was in the camp, he would have surrendered his fight for life and survival. The same can be said for Martin Luther King. If he had forgiven the men who were murdering innocent black children and women, he wouldn't have sustained his fight. There would have been a surrender. They key here is the word "fight." When someone is stripping you of your humanity, the evolved way to fight back is to hold firm and sustain your dignity. It is a peaceful protest. You are enduring the attack, but you are not surrendering to it, nor are you retaliating. If you forgive too soon, you will surrender. Wait until the attack is over, and then forgive.

CHAPTER 10

Research on Emotional Health, Emotional Intelligence and Emotional Compatibility

The most recent research done on emotional health, emotional intelligence, and emotional compatibility support the idea that emotionally evolved people are more successful at work, in their relationships, and with their health. Yet, none of these domains have been explicitly defined or articulated. Perhaps this is why finding an emotionally healthy or available partner eludes people so drastically. If it were easy to find an emotionally healthy individual, the divorce rate would be well under fifty percent.

Traditionally, emotional health has been defined as the absence of mental illness or a state of psychological well-being. Unfortunately, this definition is as helpful as describing the color pink as "the absence of blue and a lighter shade of red." It sheds some general light on what emotional health is, but it does not begin to explain it. Also, every human being experiences anxiety and depression. In fact, in mild states, they may be reoccurring symptoms in a healthy person's life. The same can be said about feelings of insecurity. Every human being has mild insecurities, and when a person accepts their insecurities and admits them, in a way that doesn't excuse bad behavior, they are healthy.

The other problem with the definition is that very sick people fake emotional health very well. Personality disordered people, and they are a dime a dozen, use pathological projection to appear uber confident and rid themselves of profound insecurities. I rarely have a bully, emotional abuser, or toxic client sitting across from me because they believe their hardships are due to other people. They feel no responsibility for their own unhappiness because they are too busy blaming others. A person who takes responsibility for their own happiness and is willing to look in the mirror is the person that lands in the chair across from a therapist, in most, if not all cases.

The emotional health of an emotionally evolved person can be extremely impaired when they become involved with an emotionally unevolved or toxic person. They can feel extreme anxiety and intense shame at times. Often, they have persistent feelings of ineptness and incompetence. Occasionally, they have a breakdown. Unfortunately, as described in previous chapters, their partner takes advantage of these situations and uses them as evidence that their partner is emotionally unstable or even mentally ill.

The studies on emotional intelligence are clear cut. Emotionally intelligent individuals are more successful at work, in their relationships, and with their health. They have a higher income bracket. For example, 98% of the top performers, professionally, are high in emotional intelligence. In addition, Emotional Intelligence is the strongest predictor of performance.

Although many emotionally unevolved individuals rise to the top because of their unscrupulous and bullying styles, frequently, their narcissism gets the best of them at some point, and they make a mistake which sheds light of their real character. Yet, an emotionally intelligent individual usually has a long and fruitful career.

The research on emotional compatibility stresses the importance of shared values. Investment in the relationship is also essential.

Cooperation and conflict resolution are equally important. On the surface, many of these qualities are misperceived if they not evaluated at a deeper level. For example, shared values. Most individuals in a committed relationship value similar things or they would not have gone on the second or third date. A woman who desperately wants children and a family is probably not going to invest in a relationship with a man who doesn't want to get married or have kids. She might spend time with this partner while looking elsewhere, but her commitment level is low. Another example includes a man who wants to retire and move to Canada. He might not invest in a relationship with a woman who has roots in the Midwest and wants to stay close to her family.

In essence, shared values are a given if the relationship has solidified. Yet, the deceptive element regarding shared values is that they are extremely general. Most people value family, working hard, faithfulness, loyalty, and honesty as important values. However, if you are with someone who is unevolved, they believe they hold these values close, but their personality construct distorts their perception of these values and the appropriate personal execution of these values.

For example, Russ values honesty, but because of his personality structure, his narcissism distorts his reality. So, Russ unknowingly changes his experience of life events to suit his cause. For example, Russ was enraged that his wife filed for divorce. As a result, he felt entitled to attempt to brainwash his kids against his wife, because he felt that he was the victim and, thus, entitled to seek revenge. He distorted stories of his wife so graphically that any kernel of truth was barely recognizable. Yet, he believed every story he told. An unevolved personality believes their distortions to be true because their defense mechanisms have altered the correct version of reality. An unevolved individual will go to their grave believing their own unique version of reality even if it directly contradicts with evidence to the contrary.

Research indicates that the second important aspect of emotional compatibility is shared investment in the relationship. Again, if evaluated on the surface, distinct characteristics of mutual investment can be identified. Examples are faithfulness and a progression from dating exclusively to engagement and marriage. The deeper issue here is that an unevolved personality will invest quickly to attempt to manipulate the situation, so their partner is dependent on them. Insecure at their foundation, they want to make it hard for their partner to ever leave them, so they are nice and kind until they can convince their partner to give up many of their own resources. Asking their partner to move away with them is one common tactic. Persuading their partner to give up their own hobbies and pursuits because they are "taking away" from their relationship is another common strategy. Sabotaging their friendships or relationships with family members also plays a role in facilitating dependence. Occasionally, they will take control of financial resources, as well. Once they have secured their partner, they often revert back to their real self.

The couple's ability to resolve conflict is also a major component of emotional compatibility. An unevolved partner will often "play nice" until the relationship is secured. Once they believe they have their partner committed and dependent, however, having a discussion with them is a bit like banging your head against the wall. No matter how many times or ways you describe your viewpoint, if your partner disagrees, he or she will not veer from their stance. There is little open-mindedness and extreme rigidity of thought. They believe their viewpoint is correct, and they won't even consider another. In addition, as discussed in earlier chapters, if you go to them with hurt feelings or discontent about something they did, they will not accept it. They will turn the situation back around on you and blame you. So, conflicts within the relationship rarely get resolved.

CHAPTER 11

Sex and Love

Nobody wants to have sex with someone who disrespects them. In fact, it's hard to like someone who continually disrespects you and how you feel. Anger, distrust, and resentment grow daily. This explains why so many people have no sex drive. Often, it's not a medical condition. They are simply tied to a selfish and unevolved person who doesn't actually deserve them or intimate relations with them.

Yet, if your relationship is caring, trusting, and close, the chances of your sex life being satisfying increases dramatically. Why? Because this is what love is. Love is emotional and physical. The mind and body are connected, whether we like it or not, and if we have to shut off our mind to have sex with our partner, it feels terrible. If our mind loves our partner, it is not difficult for our body to follow. When both the mind and body are engaged in physical intimacy, it is fulfilling, satisfying and fun.

When sex becomes an obligation in a relationship it is dysfunctional. For example, when one person demands it as their right, the other person often feels like an object or commodity. Like somehow their body is partly owned by someone else and this person has the right to have control over it when they want. In addition, they also feel like they are only a vehicle for their partners satisfaction and are tossed away after sex like a used prophylactic.

Moreover, when one partner uses sex to get what they want, they are objectifying themselves to gain a superficial desire. Because they are not authentically into the interaction, they often make their partner feel used also. Sex should not be a business transaction. It should be delightful. It should make people feel alive instead of dead. If it doesn't, there might not be enough emotional closeness in the relationship.

The final note on sex and love is that unevolved partners are often extremely selfish. They are invested in their own satisfaction. If they try and please their partner, they often try to do things they think will help their partner, but they are incapable of listening to what their partner really wants. Again, they are only able to consider what they think. This theme might run through the relationship continually, and not only in the bedroom. The unevolved partner often gives gifts they think their partner should like instead of listening to what their partner actually does like. The same can be said for surprises, dates, picking movies, and planning vacations. The unevolved person constantly plans what they think their partner should like, according to them, instead of understanding what their partner actually likes.

CHAPTER 12

Morality

Morality is the final avenue to explore when deciphering whether your partner is evolved emotionally or not. Morality is not whether someone believes in a higher power or attends church, synagogue, or any other sort of organized religious event. In fact, religion has very little to do with a person's moral maturity.

Lawrence Kohlberg identifies six levels of moral evolution, yet they are be broken down into three: pre-conventional, conventional, and post-conventional. The Pre-conventional level of moral reasoning is common in children, although many adults function at this level, as well. An individual's focus is on the direct consequences of their actions on themselves. "The last time I did that I got fined, so I won't do it again." The worse the punishment for the act, the worse the act is perceived. It is egocentric and lacking recognition that other points of view may differ from their own. There is deference to superior power or prestige because their concern is on how this power impacts them. So, in essence, they do avoid doing hurtful and destructive deeds because there will be undesirable consequences for them, not because they have empathy for the person that was hurt.

In addition, Kohlberg designates the "what's in it for me" attitude as common in the pre-conventional stage of moral development. The individual's self-interest supersedes their ability to think about what might help other people, and they only consider the act "right" if it brings them a good outcome. "As a result, concern for others is not based on loyalty or intrinsic respect, but rather a, 'I'll scratch your back, you scratch mine' type of mentality," according to Kohlberg.

When people function at this level in a relationship, Kohlberg defines them as destructive. There are not many external checks and balances in a relationship, and if the unevolved party has already manipulated the couple's environment to give themselves control over the couple's resources, there may be no consequence outside of the evolved person's discontent, which they don't care much about.

The second stage of morality defined by Kohlberg defined is the Conventional stage. This stage is typical of adolescents and adults. "To reason in a conventional way is to judge the morality of actions by comparing them to society's views and expectations. It is characterized by an acceptance of society's conventions concerning right and wrong. So, an individual obeys rules and follows society's norms even when there are no consequences for obedience and disobedience. Adherence to rules and conventions is fairly rigid, and a rule's appropriateness or fairness is seldom questioned." In essence, morality is still dictated by outside forces and the importance of being a good person is largely shaped by societies definition, meaning they follow right from wrong according to with their culture's espouses.

Thus, individuals may make blanket generalizations and judgments without evaluating the situation at a more critical and specific level. For example, divorce is wrong. Infidelity is wrong. Homosexuality is wrong. Instead of understanding the nuances of a situation, they adhere to what their culture deems right and wrong. Their need to be viewed as a "good person," drives their motivation to follow societies' guidelines. Unfortunately, this often gives unevolved individuals a license to claim they are morally superior to others because they feel reinforced by society. Moreover, this is detrimental when involved with an unevolved personality who already has inflated sense of self-importance. When backed by their culture's perception of what a good person is, for example, a good job, works hard, pays taxes, and is reasonably nice to people, they quickly disregard their partner's complaints that they are insensitive and manipulative in the relationship. According to them, because they are a "good person" as defined by society, it is easy to dismiss their partner's complaints as "crazy" and "oversensitive."

Kohlberg identified the third stage of morality as the Post-Conventional stage:

"Also called the principled level, this stage is marked by a growing realization that individuals are separate entities from society and that the individual's own perspective may take precedence over society's views; individuals may disobey rules inconsistent with their own principles. Post-convention moralists live by their own ethical principles—principles that typically include such fundamental human rights such as life, liberty, and justice. People who exhibit post-conventional morality view rules as useful, but changeable, mechanisms—ideally rules can maintain the general social order and protect human rights. Rules are not absolute dictates that must be obeyed without question."

Kohlberg

Examples of individuals who function at the post-conventional level of morality include Mother Teresa, Gandhi, and Martin Luther King.

In essence, human life and human dignity are the most important values. For example, maybe their religion and culture condemn homosexuality, but an individual in stage three places more importance on human life and human dignity. Thus, they dismiss their culture's values regarding this issue. In essence, human life and dignity trump all other values. The child or adolescent at this stage of development is the one that stands up for the different kid on the playground that is being humiliated by the rest of his class. It is the young adolescent girl who stops her friend from maliciously gossiping about a girl from another clique. It is the young adult who gives the homeless person on the bus his seat. It is the man who divorces his wife because she mistreats and bullies him and his children.

Because the unevolved personality goes to great lengths to appear morally evolved, it is not authentic because their personality construct is rooted in ego-centrism. Meaning, they engage in compassionate acts in front of others, but would not if they did not have an audience. Thus, a morality test might help elucidate where they are on the morality spectrum.

There are many conflicting cultural values included in this scenario to camouflage the correct answer. Also, the example may be personal for individuals who have lost a loved one who was in the line of duty. An apology is extended to anyone who is hurt or confused by this exercise.

The scenario includes three high ranking and specialized soldiers on a mission in a foreign country. Their mission was compromised when two female civilians accidently stumbled upon them. The soldiers who were American and had young families at home knew that if they allowed the civilians to go free, they would alert the enemy, and the soldiers had little chance of making it out of enemy territory alive. Although they appeared similar in ethnicity to the enemy, the civilians were unarmed and did not pose an immediate threat to the soldiers. Also, because of the extreme conditions of the terrain, the soldiers were aware that if they tied the civilians up to buy more time to escape, they would die within hours because of the extreme temperatures and the prevalence of wolves in the area. Another factor involved in the situation was that the enemy desecrated their prisoner's dead bodies, which sickened the soldiers who feared their wives and loved ones would suffer because of this.

The soldiers had two choices.
Shoot the civilians in order to escape alive.
Let the civilians go and face the enemy with no chance of escape, and
  inevitable death.

Some individuals choose to shoot the enemy. Their reasons might include the enemy, and the civilians were terrorists and murderers, and they need to be extinguished. The American soldiers are brave, honorable, American men who have young families to take care of. If they shoot the civilians, they are most likely saving future American lives. This may and may not be true.

Some individuals believe that the civilians, although possibly affiliated with the enemy, are still human beings who were innocently going about their business. They most likely have small children and families at home themselves. They did not attack or threaten the soldiers, so they are rather innocent in this situation. Their lives have meaning and worth, as well. Therefore, if you murder the civilians, you are no different from a terrorist. In fact, you are the exact definition of a terrorist.

In cases of self-defense, violence is warranted. If the civilians had been armed and had attempted to assassinate, the soldiers, there shouldn't be a question of whether the soldiers should shoot. The same can be said for an intruder entering your home or a mugger on the street. In these instances, human beings have every reason to fight and defend themselves by any means necessary. Yet, when innocent people are attacked because they have been framed as a threat, there is a monumental problem.

The belief that a human being is more honorable and has more value because of their nationality, education level, or religious affiliation or any other quality un-indicative of character, is all right to some extent, unless you place yourself at higher value than others because of these qualities and then feel entitled to strip them of their humanity.

Moreover, gossip, propaganda, and hateful generalizations are destructive and dangerous to all human beings. Powerful people effectively manipulate other people by playing on their fears and conjuring up a bad guy to blame. Historically, this tactic has caused more violent atrocities against human beings than any other psychological phenomenon. Human beings cannot allow the bullies of the world to reign anymore. It's time for the heroes to step up.

When this type of "I'm better than you" mentality occurs within a couple or the parent-child dyad, one person is continually humiliated and shamed. Their dignity is slowly and methodically eroded along with their identity. Avoiding this type of relationship is paramount in decreasing the divorce rate, rates of anxiety and depression, and the prevalence of personality disorders in our culture.

CHAPTER 13

Relationships Are Work

The phrase "relationships are work" is not exactly correct. Relationships do require work, but the amount of work required should not override the satisfaction derived from being in the relationship. Contrary to popular opinion, a relationship is not a job. It is supposed to be the one area in a person's life that brings about caring, love, fun, and cooperation. If the relationship seems like work, so much so that it is overwhelming and draining, the relationship may be dysfunctional. . . . meaning one person may be emotionally unavailable.

Several signs exist when a person feels like their relationship is more work than pleasure. The first is an imbalance of workload in the relationship. For example, when one person in the relationship is left with most of the work regarding the relationship, like planning and scheduling time together, taking care of most of the shared household responsibilities, parenting, and sacrificing things they used to enjoy in order to take care of the shared responsibilities, there is an imbalance of work. Most likely, the other person floats through time, doing what they want to do without much regard for the other person or the relationship. So, one person works much harder and invests more time and energy into the relationship while their partner skates by without much care or concern. Logically, this is a red flag.

This is a tricky situation because when the person doing all of the "relationship work" becomes tired and discouraged and mentions this to their partner. There is usually an uproar. As stated in previous chapters, an evolved person is thoughtful and selfless, so they are usually the relationship workhorse of the couple. When it becomes too much, and they bring these feelings to an unevolved partner, the unevolved partner has a tit for tat attitude—the second sign that the relationship has become more work than pleasure. Indignant and insulted that their partner feels this way, they highlight everything they do for their partner. They also blame their partner for demanding their time or being a nag about responsibilities. The evolved person, usually, then believes the skewed dynamic is their fault and blames themselves.

Let's take Mika and Larry for example. After several years of marriage, Mika found herself shouldering most of the household chores. Although her husband would agree to take care of some of the housework, it never got done. Yet, when Mika reminded her husband of the work that he agreed to do that wasn't getting done, he yelled at her and accused he of being a "nag" and "OCD." Eventually, she stopped asking him because of his hurtful response. The amount of housework became overwhelming, so she again asked her husband for help. Larry became enraged and told Mika that it was her job to complete all of the household duties because he worked more than she did. He indicated that he felt like "all he did was work to bring money home for her." And, although Mika was in dental school full time and also worked a part-time job to help make ends meet because Larry was the "bread winner" he felt she needed to compensate by doing the housework.

Also, an unevolved person keeps score, so to speak. They maintain a mental tally sheet. It is not because they have carried the relationship for a while and are tired, as the evolved personality sometimes is, it is a legit-imate trait in their personality. They believe if they do something for someone, they are entitled to expect a return, and continually operate on this belief. Because of their egocentric personality structure, they expe-rience anything they do for someone else as an imposition and expect the favor to be returned. At times, they appear gracious, but if a favor isn't returned in a timely fashion, they become agitated and irritated. Moreover, when they do something selfless for someone else, they like to advertise it. They will flaunt it every opportunity they receive.

Because the unevolved personality keeps score in the relationship and continually highlights their contributions, the emotionally avail-able partner is left with two choices. One, reiterate what they do to defend themselves, or, two, believe that they are the weaker character in the relationship as the emotionally unevolved person wants them to believe. Unfortunately, if they choose to defend themselves, a tit for tat fight ensues, which never ends well, or they begin to think they are the selfish and controlling person in the relationship when the opposite is actually true.

Many of these conflicts result in the emotionally available person feeling like they are banging their head against the wall, which is the third sign the relationship has become more work than pleasure. This is a result of the emotionally unevolved personality's inability to see their partner's perspective. They are only able to see, consider, and operate from their own perspective and opinion. Although the emotionally evolved partner tries to explain their perspective a zillion times over and in a trillion different ways, it falls on deaf ears. Although their partner may defend or support their partner's perspective to others outside the relationship, they are unable to accept it within the relationship if it differs from their own.

An emotionally evolved person, on the other hand, might be resistant to understanding their partner's perspective at first because they are defensive, but eventually soften and try to understand their partner's position, even if it differs from their own. It does not take them long to grasp their partner's perspective and move towards a compromise.

Take Emma and Dan for example. While they were dating, Emma casually invited Dan over, last minute, on a Saturday evening. He agreed, but a few minutes later she texted him that her kids had come home expectantly. Unsure of what to do, he remained at the restaurant where some of his friends had gathered. A while later he asked her if he should come over. Emma was torn because she knew she'd be busy with her kids, but she wanted Dan to come over, so she left it up to him. After some time had passed, Emma asked Dan if he was coming over. Dan said it was getting really late, and he needed to head home. Emma was hurt and disappointed. The next day she told Dan she was hurt he didn't come over because they wouldn't be seeing each other for a while due to schedule conflicts. Dan apologized and said he really wanted to come over, but he was afraid to drive because he had several drinks. Although Emma had been hurt and disappointed, she realized Dan had done the responsible thing. He lived across town and it was not safe for him to drink and drive. She also realized she had been wishy-washy with her last minute invitation, and that was probably the reason Dan had remained at the restaurant with his friends. . . . Because he was waiting for some direction.

This example looks different when there is an emotionally unevolved person involved. Let's say Emma has an unevolved personality structure. She would not be able to consider Dan's position. She would remain hurt and angry and blame Dan for being selfish. Most likely she would accuse Dan of putting his friends first. Unable to put herself in Dan's shoes, she would blame him for the incident and remain angry and self-righteous. If Dan apologized and attempted to explain his position further to help Emma understand that it was not that he did not want to come over, it was that it was not safe, Emma would be unable to consider his perspective and continue to reiterate that he is selfish and he puts his friends first. Because Emma is not open to thinking about Dan's position the night before, his explanation continues to fall on deaf ears and the argument feels a little like Dan is beating his head against the wall because there is no understanding, compromise, or cooperative effort to resolve a confusing situation.

If Dan had the unevolved personality structure, the argument would, again, have little resolution. . . . similar to the feeling of banging your head against the wall. For example, when Emma acknowledges she is hurt that he did not come over the night before, Dan would argue that she gave a last minute invitation, planned poorly because her kids came home, and was wishy-washy. He would infer she was a poor planner and communicator, and if she wanted him to come over in the future, she needs to be clear. After all, he's not a mind reader. When Emma reiterates that she did not know her kids were coming home and that she wanted Dan to WANT to come over because she was worried about their ability to entertain both parties, Dan ignores her explanation and reiterates his own again. Now, Emma is left feeling worse than before, and her perspective is tossed out the window.

In essence, a relationship should never feel like a job. There are times, perhaps when a spouse gets sick or injured, and one partner ends up shouldering most of the couple's responsibilities, which is necessary, but on a day to day basis, both partners should feel like they are part of a two person team. Where things get done without much delegation, counting, effort or fighting. A partner who continually keeps track of what they do for the other is also trouble. This, "Look at what I do for you, you owe me," is an immature attitude which negates any chance of cooperation, trust or equality in the relationship. It is utilized when one partner wants to excuse their shortcomings or make the other person in the relationship feel guilty and less than.

Essentially when there are two emotionally evolved people in a relationship, their ability to see their partner's perspective, even if it differs from their own, in addition to their tendency to derive pleasure in doing something selfless for someone else, allows them to tackle shared responsibilities efficiently and without much conflict. Of course, there is always some mild discontent about getting mundane tasks done, and, in a healthy couple, probably some good-natured teasing about these tasks, but, for the most part, they happen pretty naturally.

A relationship is dysfunctional when the following dynamics are present: there is an apparent imbalance in the workload, one person has a tit for tat attitude, and one person feels like they are banging their head against the wall because their opinion or perspective is never taken into consideration if it opposes their partner's. In these cases, it is important to consider whether your partner is emotionally unevolved and if they are, if counseling would help.

CHAPTER 14

The Burning Question

S o, the question that most, if not all, emotionally available people ask regarding their emotionally unavailable partner is, "Do they know what they are doing?" Or, "Are they aware of what they are doing?" This is an exceedingly difficult question to answer and has several explanations and repercussions. If we believe they are innocent and don't have control over their behavior, it is easier to remain in a relationship with them. So, which is it? The answer is, a little of both.

Yes, in most cases, they are aware of their cruelness, but, and this is the complicated part, they feel justified in their actions. They feel entitled to treat their partner the way they do because they believe their partner deserves that treatment. In their mind, they are doing the right thing because it is just punishment. It is almost similar to a teacher feeling entitled to punish a child that is doing something wrong. An unevolved person feels that teaching their partner the correct way to be in a relationship is their right and their job.

In addition, the unevolved person doesn't want to be bothered by their partner's opinions and feelings. They only actually care about their own opinions and being gratified. For an emotionally unevolved person, this usually involves superficial gratifiers such as money, status, and sex. Sometimes, if their children are a source of ego gratification for them, it is their children. For example, a son who is the star quarterback on the football team might get a lot of his parents' attention because they enjoy the status it gives them. Because an unevolved personality perceives themselves as more important than their partner, they do not care about their partner's feelings or opinions, and easily and readily dismisses them. Occasionally they might give lip service to them in front of other people, but behind closed doors, they dismiss and ignore their partner's needs. In many cases, they act irritated and annoyed that their partner might even attempt to express their opinion.

In essence, an unevolved person is aware that they are cruel and dismissive to their partner, but they feel justified in doing so. They sincerely believe their partner deserves this treatment, and are very good at convincing others, including their partner, of the same. Of course all of their personality traits discussed so far, such as their lack of empathy, vindictive nature, tendency to externalize blame and belief that their way is the right way and the only way, contribute to the continuous belief that they are either the honorable party in their romantic relationship and, thus, entitled to control and dominate their partner, or they are the victim in their relationship and, therefore, allowed to retaliate and act cruelly.

Of course, this perception of themselves, their partner, and the relationship is distorted. It is the mirror opposite of their emotionally evolved partner's perception, which is why the opportunity to repair the relationship is difficult. In an emotionally unavailable person's eyes, they don't do much wrong because their behaviors and responses are warranted.

This is exceedingly difficult for an emotionally healthy person to comprehend, because acting vindictively, unempathicly, and selfishly is against their nature and feels exceptionally wrong to them. It is hard for them to understand how their emotionally unevolved partner can excuse and defend these tendencies as if they are honorable.

In worst case scenarios, when an emotionally unavailable partner is pathological—meaning their pathological tendencies, such as lack of empathy, narcissism, spitefulness, and victim mentality, are extreme, they are not aware of their cruelty. In fact, they utilize the defense mechanism denial to erase their abhorrent acts from their awareness. In these situations, it is necessary for the emotionally evolved partner to exit the relationship in order to keep themselves and their children safe.

So how does an emotionally available partner proceed when there is some awareness on their partner's behalf? The answer is thoughtfully and carefully. Unfortunately, many emotionally healthy people tie themselves to an emotionally unhealthy partner, and they convince themselves that the discontent and disconnect they feel in the relationship is mild. After all, most emotionally evolved individuals find happiness and satisfaction in many other relationships and endeavors, so feeling dissatisfied in one relationship should not be a reason to leave. Moreover, if leaving their partner means divorce and breaking up their family, they feel leaving their partner because of their own unhappiness is selfish.

However, there are a few consequences with remaining in the relationship. The first is the impact on an emotionally healthy person's self-esteem. When someone consistently dismisses a person's feelings, disrespects them, and strips them of their dignity, it has a dehumanizing effect. In other words, they are taking away the only things that truly qualifies a person as human, leaving the person feeling less than, worthless, and ashamed of themselves. Initially, there is no other response but anger when someone experiences this treatment. In fact, rage might be a more accurate description. And, when an emotionally healthy person feels anger and rage quite a bit, they feel ashamed and out of control which causes them to lose sight of the original offense and condemn themselves. Continuously experiencing this cycle often causes depression, anxiety, and a compromised self-esteem.

In fact, over the course of years, this treatment can demoralize the person to the extent that they lose their identity. As terrible as it sounds, they sometimes end up surrendering to their partner's beliefs and taking on their perspective. The crime in this situation is that a vital, compassionate, empathic member of society, who is a humanitarian and contributes to peace and love in this world, is stripped of their health and spirit by their partner. The world needs good people running it, not egomaniacs.

The second repercussion when deciding to remain with an emotionally unevolved person is the impact on the children. Although the children get most of their deep and complicated emotional needs met from their emotionally healthy parent, two dynamics work against the healthy parent and can wreak havoc. The first dynamic is the emotionally unavailable parent's display of power in front of the children. Because they are narcissistic, they love to show off their power and dominate family life. They position themselves as the boss. In subtle ways, they exploit power over the emotionally unevolved person to ensure the kids see who is really the powerful one. Often they flaunt their status, money, or power in front of the children.

Unfortunately, this tactic works exceptionally well for most children. Children are enamored with power because often they feel small and powerless in a big world filled with big people. This is why they have superheroes and princesses as heroes. A psychological defense mechanism exists which describes this phenomenon. It is called identifying with the aggressor. Most of the time, when children are faced with a traumatic or conflicting situation, they often identify with the aggressor rather than the victim. This is because a child already feels small and powerless in the face of a scary situation, so identifying with the victim makes them feel even more terrified. Identifying with the aggressor, however, alleviates anxiety because they borrow the aggressor's power by identifying them and emulating them.

Thus, when a child is being parented by an emotionally available parent and an emotionally unavailable parent, even though they are closer to the emotionally available parent, they will still identify and desire the emotionally unavailable parent because of their purposeful display of power. When they idealize this parent, they also begin to exploit their power against the emotionally available parent, which is devastating to be treated poorly by both their spouse and their child.

In addition, identifying with and idealizing with an emotionally unavailable parent is not the healthiest choice, psychologically, for the child. Every parent wants a secure, happy, child who is a good person. Emotionally unavailable people are not happy unless they being superficially gratified, and a life filled with superficial gratification is not an actually full, satisfying or authentically happy life. Also, your child will either marry an emotionally unavailable partner and be treated poorly, or they will end up being an emotionally unavailable partner and treat their spouse and children poorly.

The second dynamic that exists when an emotionally healthy and an emotionally unhealthy couple raise children is that the emotionally unhealthy parent is continuously jealous of the joy the healthy parent experiences when they are with their child. And, because they have a jealous and vindictive nature, tend to attempt to sabotage their partner's relationship with their child or children. One of the ways they accomplish this is setting up the other parent to be the villain. Often they will make sarcastic comments or subtly put their partner down in front of the child, as well. Over time, these tactics, erode the child's perception of the healthy parent.

Making the decision to leave an emotionally unhealthy partner has its share of fallout, and needs to be done with the awareness that the unhealthy partner will be enraged that their partner is leaving and will be exceedingly vindictive. In many cases, the emotionally unhealthy partner talks maliciously behind their healthy partner's back to get the community against the healthy partner. When this happens, it is so painful and terrible and unfair, that it is difficult for the healthy partner to endure. The unhealthy partner will distort most of what the healthy partner does and broadcast it maliciously to anyone and everyone that will listen. And, unfortunately, because they are effective manipulators, they usually succeed in aligning people against the healthy partner.

The unhealthy partner, because of their vindictive character and unscrupulous nature, will most likely use the kids to hurt the healthy partner. The attempt to turn the children against the healthy partner and continually put them in the middle of arguments are two tactics an unhealthy parent utilizes during a divorce. Because they are consumed with themselves and their own feelings, they are incapable of considering how these manipulations affect the children. They feel entitled to do whatever they need to do to punish their partner for leaving them.

There are several tactics a person can employ when they are in the throes of a nasty divorce with an unhealthy partner. The first is to prepare for hurtful comments and unfair allegations. Ignore these comments. Do not engage, because the emotionally unavailable partner's goal is to hurt their partner and get a rise out of their partner. This makes them powerful. The secondary goal of the emotionally unavailable partner is to get their partner upset so they make rash decisions. Always take the time to think through your decisions. Do not surrender to your partner's demands because he is scaring you with threats or harassment. Stand strong and believe in yourself.

The third step is to attempt to catch your spouse in the act. Save their threatening and harassing emails, texts, and voicemails, and document their antics. After you've accrued a list, bring it to an attorney.

The second step is to educate your children. Saying things like, "when mom's mad, sometimes she tells stories that are not true." Explain that this is not her fault, but that it is her way of handling hurt and anger. Ask your kids to talk to talk you about things that are said that are confusing, so you can help them with their feelings.

Remaining calm and unaffected when they become nasty, documenting the volatile and inappropriate interactions, and appropriately and politely educating your children are tips that will help if or when deciding to divorce a spouse becomes a reality.

CHAPTER 15

The Emotionally Healthy Person

Although the deceptions and manipulations of an emotionally unhealthy person have been elucidated, and it is easy to see how an emotionally available person becomes involved with an emotionally unavailable person, there is more to say about the emotionally healthy person.

Because healthy people are self-aware and because all human beings have insecurities, healthy people are aware of their insecurities and sometimes believe they are flawed because they have them. This couldn't be further from the truth. Having insecurities is a human being's plight, and they are nothing to be ashamed of. Loving yourself too much is a problem. Narcissism, vanity, and arrogance are destructive tendencies that promote egocentrism and pathology. It's ok to be self-critical, and self-evaluative, and humble, yet, people often condemn these tendencies. "You think too much," or "You over analyze," are criticisms frequently conveyed to the self-reflective. Yet it is the self-reflective people in the world who are insightful and make efforts to be a better person. Looking in the mirror is a courageous and tough thing to do, and for some reason, it is under-valued.

For example, most individuals who enter therapy are, for the most part, healthy. They are taking responsibility for their lack of happiness or flaws and actively trying to help themselves. However, it is rare an emotionally unhealthy person enters therapy because they believe their problems are everyone else's fault and not their own. Often they criticize therapy and people who go to therapy, referring to them as "crazy" or "have issues." Unfortunately, this is an incorrect perception. Therapy is a health seeking behavior and should be commended and encouraged.

When an emotionally healthy person who feels that they have issues and flaws encounters an emotionally unhealthy person, they often see this person's narcissism and vanity as confidence. Because they feel less confident, they feel better being around someone who never second guesses themselves and believes they are infallible. They mistake this lack of insight for security, and being around this person, initially, makes them feel confident. But, if they accepted their insecurities and realized all emotionally healthy people have insecurities they might not make the mistake of falling for an emotionally unavailable person, who, very honestly, deserves to be with an emotionally unavailable partner like themselves.

Another issue is the way in which we are trained to view relationships and potential partners. For example, a good looking person is expected to be with a good looking partner. An uber intelligent person is expected to be with another intellectual. If things don't match up superficially, people expect other superficial qualities to make up for it. For example, it is acceptable for an unattractive man to be with an extremely attractive woman if he makes a lot of money. . . . or a super-intelligent man to be with an unintelligent woman if she is coming from a well-established family of status in the community. In other words, we place significance on the superficial aspects of a relationship and believe relationships work if these match on the surface. The aspects of a person that involve power, such as money, prestige, beauty and status are what we think people should be matched by. Perhaps that is why the divorce rate is so high.

Yet, not a lot of importance is placed on the non-superficial. Character and integrity are considered secondarily. One of the reasons for this, of course, is because character and integrity are harder to decode. Superficial qualities are easily seen and understood, so it makes sense that we use this to categorize and understand people. Yet, there might be something more. People are unnerved when an unattractive man is with a very attractive woman, or a wealthy and successful woman is with a man who has a lower level job. The couple loses some status when their superficial qualities do not match.

People can fake easily and go to great lengths to do so when they have an audience they want to impress. Again, it is analogous to a politician kissing a baby. A person's behavior behind closed doors or without an audience to impress is more likely to show their true colors. Another analogy is the manner in which a person treats their servers at a restaurant, or the custodian of their place of employment. Do they treat people in less powerful positions the same as they treat people in more powerful positions or do they decide a human beings value by their place on "the food chain."

In a great many cases. It is common for an emotionally healthy person, because they are mildly insecure, to settle for someone who might not be emotionally healthy. Sometimes this is because the emotionally unhealthy person positions themselves to appear secure and confident, but often it is because the emotionally healthy person is humble, aware of their insecurities, and, thus, feels they don't deserve better.

The aspects of ourselves that determine our worth should include humanitarianism, capacity for empathy, effort, personal accountability, sensitivity, and kindness. If we embody these characteristics and do everything possible to employ these characteristics, we deserve someone equally as wonderful. Superficial qualities such as physical appearance, money, and status are icing on an already delicious cake.

CHAPTER 16

The Mind and Body Connection

Emotional closeness and empathy are the two entities that bring about contentment, peace, and joy. Both alleviate depression and dissipate anxiety, improving the quality of life and mental health for everyone involved. They are the key to raising emotionally healthy children with a solid character who express their gifts with the world and make it a better place. When human beings are happy, they are innovative, creative, determined, tenacious, and brilliant. Although this book has described what emotional closeness is and how to get it and keep it, in addition to what empathy is and how to have it, there is a third piece that is almost as important as emotional closeness and empathy: it is the mind and body connection.

The mind and body connection is an Eastern philosophy and is practiced religiously in most Asian cultures. The belief is that the mind and body are healthiest when there is unity between the two. The state of feeling whole, grounded, and alive is the strongest when the mind and body are connected. Plus, when the mind and body are in a state of connectedness, there is little experience of anxiety and depression. Focus is astute. The term, "in the zone" articulates the mind and body connection. When the mind and body are connected, peak physical performance is achieved, as well.

Human beings feel most alive, centered, and soothed when they experience the connection and the more they practice sustaining the connection, the longer and more permanent these positive feelings remain. In this state, a human being is much more capable of emotional closeness and empathy. This is because these capabilities require an open heart and an open mind. The mind body connection primes a person for an open heart and open mind because they themselves are grounded, centered, and soothed.

An analogy would be a mother with a young child. Is she most nurturing and loving when she is stress free and rested or when she is anxious, worried, and depressed? Much research has indicated that a mother free of depression and anxiety has a more secure attachment to her child, which translates to positive developmental progressions and mental health in the child. In essence, an emotionally healthy individual increases their capacity for emotional closeness and empathy if they feel whole.

So, what is the mind and body connection? It occurs when the mind and body are working together towards a common goal. The mind has to think about what the body is doing for the body to do it. Cooperation exists between the mind and body. Traditional forms of the connection are yoga, tai chi, martial arts, and dance. Many non-traditional forms exist as well. Most sports require a mind and body connection. . . . for example, tennis, soccer, lacrosse, basketball, racquetball, etc. Creating art is a powerful mind and body connector as well. The hands become the mind's tools for expression. Painting, sculpting, and woodworking are examples. Engaging in mind and body activities as often as time allows is important, even if it is only once or twice a week.

Let's use tennis as an example of a mind and body activity. One of the most infamous books written about tennis describes the mind and body connection (although the author does not use those terms), and the importance of it. The book is titled, "The Inner Game of Tennis," and it talks about the problems that occur in tennis when the mind and body are at odds with each other.

It is common in tennis for people to reprimand themselves after missing a shot. They will say to themselves, "Bend Your Knees!" or "Top spin, you idiot!" Often, they get mad at their body for not performing as they want it to. When this happens—when the mind gets mad at the body—a division between the mind and the body is created. The division causes the body to tense up and instead of relaxing and flowing through the shot naturally like in practice, the body stiffens and second guesses itself, often stopping instead of following through or forgetting to bend at the knees because of tension and stiffness. The division widens with every shot and negativity and frustration take over. Then the body is really in trouble.

However, if the mind stays the bodies' friend instead of becoming its enemy, a different result occurs. If the mind has faith and trust in the body, the body remains relaxed and can stay fluid. Muscle memory becomes instinct, and the body naturally performs the way it is capable of performing. This is the mind and body connection. When the mind and the body cooperate and collaborate positively, wonderful things happen.

Although distance running, swimming, and biking, can help a person to feel better. Often, these exercises cause more of a division than a connection. Not every distance run releases endorphins or feels good. Frequently I hear runners talk about how difficult it was to get through their run. In these instances, the mind is yelling at the body to do what the mind wants. This creates a rift. In addition, the mind and body do not have to collaborate intricately in order to run. Many runners switch to autopilot and their mind wanders and is focused on anything but what their legs and arms are doing. Running does have a meditative effect because of the rhythmic breathing and can be soothing afterward if you run long and hard enough to release endorphins, but it is less of a mind body connecting activity than some others.

An important aspect of the mind body connection is the more a person practices it, the more it is sustained. This is why it is practiced three and four times a day in the Eastern cultures. Tai chi, martial arts, meditation, yoga, and prayer are all activities which link the mind and body and ground, soothe, and focus the individual. They are reminded of what is important and live their lives in a more grounded and conscious state.

Unfortunately, the mind and body split in the Western cultures is profound. Proof of this split is the medical model. The mind and body are treated as entirely separate entities. For example, if you have a broken bone, you go to an orthopedic doctor. If you have depression, you see a psychologist. An orthopedic doesn't ask his patient if the accident gives him nightmares or flashbacks or has clouded his spirit. Nor does a psychologist attempt to fix a broken bone. Yet, the mind and body are connected, and when the body is broken, the mind hurts, as well. And, when the mind hurts, the body suffers. This explains why psychosomatic symptoms are on the rise. It also explains why people in a great deal of emotional pain, cut or mutilate themselves. The division between the mind and body has become so great that the mind is lost. When the mind is lost from the body and vice versa, intense pain or numbness occurs. When this negative state becomes extreme often human beings attempt to force the body back to the broken mind through the experience of physical pain. Suicide is the complete severing of the mind and the body, literally. It is simply the enactment of a mind who cannot find its way back to its body, and the state is too painful to bear, so they end their life.

Anxiety is the mind's experience of the mind and body split, and physical pain is the body's experience of the mind body split. There are more medically unexplainable physical ailments now than ever before. These psychosomatic complaints abound. The same goes for anxiety. Anxiety wasn't common thirty years ago. This can be explained by the shift from an agricultural society to an industrial society. Not many people work with their hands anymore or do any type work that utilizes the mind and body simultaneously. Commercialization has replaced the handmade, and small business owners have been usurped by large corporations. We seldom walk anywhere because it's quicker to drive, and riding bikes has become newly popular but remains largely a leisurely activity instead of a way of life.

Attention Deficit Disorder is also a symptom of the mind and body split. The brain lacks a chemical which evenly regulates attention, so the mind wanders and distraction occurs. This is why people with ADD like to keep moving. It's the mind trying to find the connection to the body again, which feels relieving. Often, sports are the best medicine for someone with attention deficit disorder because it is stimulating, and provides a mind and body connection, and the more time spent in this state, the longer it is preserved without the activity.

An additional example of the pain a mind and body split can cause is eating disorders. Again, the mind is at odds with the body. The mind judges, condemns and punishes the body. Without a healthy mind and body connection, the two function alone and in isolation, which reflects exactly how the person feels. The body's cues and signals for food are ignored by the mind, and the body starves. The body retaliates by slowing down the person's metabolism, but that is the opposite of what the mind wants, so the mind fights back and withholds more food. If the split could be lessened and the mind and body connection re-established, either through traditional activities such as yoga, tai chi, martial arts, and dance or through more Americanized versions of the mind and body activities such as sports, painting, drawing, coloring, creating music, the person feels better. This is not to discount the importance of psychotherapy in the person's treatment in order to understand what series of events cause the intense shame that split the mind and body in the first place, which is equally important.

Promiscuity or sex addictions are also an example of a mind and body split. This mind and body split, which can also be understood as dissociation, causes many people to seek out constant physical gratification without the involvement of the mind. I have heard many promiscuous people admit that they don't enjoy sex, but they are compelled to seek it out for some reason. This compulsion comes from the mind, not the body, yet because a disconnect exists, the body doesn't fully understand what the mind wants and seeks out sex as a way to find what the mind wants, which is usually, emotional closeness and empathy.

Our daily routines also exemplify the mind and body split prevalent in our culture. For example, most of us sit at a desk for 8 hours a day, utilizing only our minds. Then, we head to the gym, sometimes to get on a treadmill and force our body to run while we distract our mind from the boring exercise by staring at the tv in front of our treadmill, or a magazine on our treadmill dashboard. A much healthier choice is to take a dance class, martial art class, or yoga class, where the body and mind have a chance to get re-acquainted and connected again. Any physical event that makes time feel like it passes quickly is usually a mind body connector. For example, many tennis players do not want to stop playing tennis at the end of their drill. Often, they look forward to the days they play tennis, and if it were not for physical fatigue, would play tennis all day if they could.

Another example of the mind body split prevalent in our culture pertains to sex. Often our obsession with physical appearance and isolated body parts divides the mind from the body. Often attraction is based on how large or small body parts look. Sometimes we break a person down according to their body parts. "She has lovely legs." "He has nice hair." "He has a beautiful body." We have gotten into the habit of fragmenting a person's body and evaluating it completely separate from the whole person. The term, "She's hot," is also an example. The person's value is tied to their physical appearance instead of who they are as a whole. In other words, people are objectified by the media which means their mind and spirit are dismissed, and their body is the focus of attention.

It's hard to consider these tendencies because we have been socialized from a very young age by the media to fragment people's bodies and evaluate them based on these different pieces. Again, we are not socialized to view people as a whole entity. It is rare that you hear someone say, "She is a beautiful person," or "He is an honorable man." The media highlights butts and boobs regularly. "Tits and ass" are what is highlighted on almost every magazine cover, commercial, and adult TV show. Obviously, we eventually get to character, but it is not the first thing we assign a value to when regarding a human being. It is the physical appearance or body. Because the body is evaluated before the mind when encountering a human being, there is an inevitable mind body split. Because of this initial perception, the mind and body split is furthered.

The argument can be made that we take in the physical first because of the way our brain processes information, and this is partly true, but we rarely remember a person's eye color or name after a brief initial encounter. Yet, we clearly remember their physical attributes. We have been socialized to pay attention to sexual body parts. Moreover, almost every popular song on the radio includes comments about booties. If you were an alien from outer space and listened to the popular songs on the radio, you would think all of a human being's power and worth came from the size and shape of their bootie. If this is ever to change, we must begin socializing our kids to think character is sexy not the shape and size of their anatomical parts.

As adults, the lack of emotional closeness in our romantic relationships has led to an increase in the utilization of pornography in order meet a human being's sexual needs, instead of sex with a loving partner. Unfortunately, because porn only focuses on the physical and keeps character and humanity out of the scene, it furthers the mind body split. It may be great for a physical release, but ultimately, the mind body split it perpetuates leaves people more depressed and anxious after they view it. To combat these feelings and to get a positive physical release, they need pornography again and again and again. It is like alcohol; they use it to feel better initially, but ending up feeling worse in the long run. They also need more and more of it to feel that initial feeling of satisfaction and escape.

Feelings of emotional closeness wet the sexual appetite in even the most non-sexual people. Unfortunately, emotionally unavailable people will only experience sex at a superficially gratifying act, but emotionally available individuals feel excited, passionate, comforted, soothed, nurtured, and loved through a sexual encounter with their partner. Sex bonds the couple emotionally and they develop a chemical attraction to each other. If emotional closeness is lost, so is sexual desire. A couple who doesn't enjoy sex regularly lacks emotional closeness, and the relationship may be in trouble.

Sex with a loving partner is the ultimate mind and body connection. If you are having exciting, pleasurable sex with a partner, you feel deeply connected to your partner. Your mind is completely focused on the experience. Your mind and body are cooperating with your partner's mind and body. Experiencing the mind connection with your partner who is experiencing a mind body connection, then sharing that experience is intensely pleasurable.

Another example of the mind body connection is art. A great deal of art includes nudity and sexual poses and positions. Often it includes fragmented body parts. Unlike pornography, art is an expression of the human spirit and all that it includes. Art does not merely depict a physical act, devoid of the mind and spirit; art expresses all of it. This is what distinguishes art from a picture or a drawing. Art reflects feeling and spirit. It moves people emotionally and physically.

The creation of art is also a significant mind and body connector. Painting, sculpting, writing, drawing, and woodworking are a few examples of the human hands acting as the mind's tools. The body and mind work together to create something. Unfortunately, most people have jobs that do not allow creativity. They are prescribed by their company the procedure and protocol for completing their tasks. This can be monotonous and draining; yet, it is what most human beings do. Imagine if people could create and innovate at work. There might be more excitement and joy in the workplace.

In essence, childhood pain, the way we are socialized by the media, and a lack of empathy and emotional closeness can cause a mind body split. The split grows wider every day if these experiences are not figured out. Most of the time, psychotherapy is a good way to start sorting these issues out. Immediate relief can be achieved through participating in a mind and body activity regularly.

In addition to the activities described above, meditation is also a mind and body connector. Although it is harder to master effectively, meditation is also centering, soothing, and grounding. The westernized version of meditation is prayer. Quietly saying a prayer repeatedly is a form of meditation because breathing becomes rhythmic and the body and mind slow down together to achieve focus and clarity. Many people find praying soothing and reassuring. For others, meditation is a necessity.

CHAPTER 17

Attachment and the Mind and Body Connection

The research on the quality of attachment between an infant and caregiver is definite. The more empathic and responsive the caregiver, the healthier and happier the infant. In fact, the research on infant mental health confirms the biologic instinct of an infant is to attract their caregiver in order to bond and ensure they stick around because the caregiver is necessary for the infant's survival. Crying, cooing, smiling, grasping, and eye contact are all ways the infant draws their caregiver close. If the attachment with the caregiver is tenuous, the infant is left in negative physical states for extended periods of time which causes long term distress. Hunger, coldness, wetness, and pain are all physical states in infancy that can cause the infant mental and emotional distress. If the distress lasts too long and is too intense without an empathic response from a caregiver consistently, the infant will withdraw and develop maladaptive defense mechanisms to deal with their psychological pain. If the caregiver is extremely neglectful, the child will withdraw so significantly that they will fail to thrive.

An infant's physical state is connected to their psychological well-being, and they depend on their caregivers for this. As indicated, the dependence on the caregiver is critical to their survival. In fact, infants are neurologically hardwired to attract and attach to their caregiver. Infants recognize their caregiver's voice at three months and can discriminate between their caregiver's face and another face as well. An infant's preference for their caregiver is apparent when there is a separation, or they are given a choice. The quality of attachment not only ensures an infant's mental health and proper development but the preservation of the mind and body connection.

As most parents know, caring for an infant includes a ton of physical activity. Holding, rocking, soothing touch, feeding, cradling, patting, tickling, hugging, etc., are examples. The soothing and nurturing that stems from a parent's physical relationship with their child is infinite. A parent's lap is sometimes the safest place for a little one. Physical closeness is imperative when raising a little one. The sensations the child's body feels soothes their mind, and when their bodies feel comforted, their mind does as well.

If this sort of physical nurturing is absent from a child's life, often they become anxious and depressed. As the child grows older, the frequency of hugs and cuddling is less. Play and activity become a way to fill this need. When a child plays, their mind and body are one. Research has indicated that play is the cornerstone of proper cognitive development and emotional and psychological health. The play is a mind and body activity.

As the child progresses through adolescence, their body changes and becomes a bit unfamiliar. At these times, it is not uncommon for the mind and body split to widen and girls and boys can become preoccupied with how their body looks. Often critical and sometimes ashamed of their body looks, the mind and body split widens and anxiety intensifies. If not retrieved the anxiety and depression can become significant and self-harm and suicidal tendencies become a reality. Teen suicide and cutting have reached a new high in this country. A teenager's anger and frustration with their body often leads them to be reckless with it. They intoxicate their bodies and disrespect their bodies by becoming promiscuous or careless with it. At these times, it is imperative to help the young person re-establish the connection because they are in pain.

In adulthood, although adults become more accepting of their bodies, the physical sensations that connect the mind and the body are largely absent, and without activities that connect the two, they will suffer from a split. As described, human beings need physical touch that is nurturing and loving. We walk through our adult lives without a whole lot of it. Often people are in long term relationships where hugging, kissing, and mutually pleasurable intercourse is not a regular occurrence. Without physical affection and love, the mind and body split widens, and anxiety and stress take over.

A study done on attachment highlights physical touch and nurturing as not only a need essential to a human being's mental health but survival. The study was conducted by psychologist Harry Harlow at The University of Wisconsin in the 1950s, and is frequently referred to as, "The Monkey Love Experiments." Although the experiment utilized monkeys, the study was extrapolated to human beings and became a foundation for attachment studies and infant mental health and development.

Harlow separated infant monkeys from their mothers and placed each with a surrogate mother. The surrogate mothers were machines that dispensed milk, yet, one mother was made out of bare wire mesh, and the other had a soft terry cloth blanket draped over it and secured to it. Harlow's first significant observation was that when given the choice of mothers, the infant monkeys sought comfort and clung to the terry-cloth mother, even when their physical nourishment came from bottles mounted on the bare wire mothers. This suggested that an infant's love was not just based on the fulfillment of their biological need. That the soft and close physical touch was equally as important as fulfilling a biological need. The research was immediately applied to infants and the knowledge that an infant's relationship with their mother and the importance of nurturing and soothing physical contact was found to be imperative to an infant's mental health.

A second finding which furthered this idea stemmed from the observations of the orphanages in the 1990s in Romania. Unfortunately, the conditions were dire, and none of the infants were held, interacted with, or had any positive stimulation. The children were warehoused in metal cribs and naked and cold without human interaction, toys, books, or even any color on the walls. Some of these children were adopted by families in the United States, and within a few years, it was discovered that the early deprivation and neglect not only had an impact on their physical and emotional development, but it damaged them neurologically. Brain scans showed dark pockets in their brain, absent of brain activity. Essentially, parts of these children's brains never developed and the brain matter died because there was no positive stimulation for too many years. Positive stimulation, from nurturing physical touch, interaction, play and love from a consistent caregiver is what promoted healthy brain development in infants, as well as physical and emotional health.

The findings of both of these discoveries were conclusive, an infant's mind and body thrive if they are cared for by a consistent caregiver with whom they develop a secure attachment. This attachment dictates the infant's ability to trust and love for the remainder of their lives. It is referred to as a working attachment. If an infant has a secure attachment to a caregiver in infancy, they are likely to have a healthy attachment style with their romantic partner in adulthood.

Secondly, the absolute importance of the mind and body connection is demonstrated by these studies, as well. Infants are happiest when they have this connection. At first, they need their caregiver to solidify this connection. The caregiver helps the infant connect with their body and regulate physical sensations. They change the infant when the infant is wet, swaddle the infant when the infant is cold, feed the infant when the infant is hungry. Through loving touch, eye contact and voice inflection, they help the baby engage with their body and utilize it to walk, play, run, and learn. Essentially, they learn through their caregiver how to solidify this mind and body connection. If they lose the connection and there is a split, and the mind perishes and body suffers.

Children are able, through play, to sustain this mind body connection. Play is the way a child's mind continues to grow and evolve. It is critical for neurological functioning, emotional health, and physical development. It is the foundation for creativity, social connection, feelings of self-efficacy, and innovation. Play is a mind and body connection.

Yet, as humans get older, the time and space to play become less. In adolescence, the changes in the body combined with messages from the media, a lack of emotional closeness with their parents, and certain life events that have caused the intense adolescent shame, can cause a split. A split in the mind body connection causes anxiety, depression, and the compulsion to self-harm. By inflicting pain on themselves, they are forcing their mind back to their body because pain, at the very least, is a bodily sensation. Having any physical sensation is better than feeling numb.

In adulthood, the absence of play and activities that connect the mind and the body, combined with an emersion in a culture where this split is the norm, and a lack of emotional closeness and physical intimacy also cause a split. The split causes anxiety, depression, and a constant need for superficial physical stimulation either from pornography, substance abuse, or shopping. These superficial activities get the blood pumping and adrenaline and endorphins are temporarily released, but they are devoid of any substance, so the good feelings are fleeting and are replaced by feelings of shame and self-loathing shortly after.

We can extrapolate from infant mental health and say, conclusively, that the mind and body connection is essential to a human being's survival. It is equally important in adolescence adulthood. Even the elderly prove this point. Those in the geriatric population that stay active, both mind and body, remain healthy and happy. It is clear that the mind and body need to stay connected throughout the lifespan for a person to be happy and healthy. The more one can engage in these activities; the more the connection is preserved and sustained. So, play as much tennis as you want. Take time to paint or draw. Do some yoga, and play with your children. When the mind and body are connected, there is more of a chance for emotional closeness, and empathy. All three of these things create happiness and well-being for a person.

CHAPTER 18

The Mind and Body Connection and Emotionally Unavailable People

eople feel whole and alive when the mind and body are connected, and this feeling allows them to access the essence of who they are. The connection puts a person in touch with himself. The sense of knowing who you are is the result of a healthy mind and body connection. An emotionally healthy person seems to have a spirit about them that is unique and special. It is a selfless, thoughtful, and compassionate spirit. This is the opposite of a person who has narcissistic tendencies. A person who is only concerned with the gratification of their ego through superficial means. Narcissists make up a large population of the emotionally unavailable pool, and most emotionally unavailable people are consumed with attention, money, success, and admiration. Moreover, their seemingly selfless gestures or acts of charity do not originate from a genuine place, but rather as a mechanism to create a favorable impression with people they want to impress. In other words, they only attempt selflessness when they have an audience or can advertise it.

Using a pool as an analogy, the emotionally unavailable person's depth is 6 feet, while an emotionally healthy person's pool is 12 feet deep. This explains why the emotionally unavailable person does not understand more profound thoughts and feelings. Their pool does not run that deep. They are chiefly concerned with their own gratification. Which explains why an emotionally unavailable person is incapable of empathy—because they cannot see beyond their own nose.

Unfortunately, an emotionally unavailable person has some awareness that an emotionally healthy person has a powerful essence about them. Yet, they don't understand this essence because they place importance on superficial aspects of a person. The idea that power can come from something other than money, status, success, or beauty, is lost on them. They are attracted to it at first because it is appealing, yet, as time goes by, it becomes a reminder of who they are not. Because emotionally unavailable people are extremely jealous and are profoundly insecure, which they lack insight to, they are deeply threatened by this mysterious power that they do not possess. So, they must dominate and control it, and because they lack the capacity for insight, they act on this aggression without awareness.

As stated previously, an emotionally unavailable person attacks their partner's identity with devaluing put-downs. The criticisms are disrespectful and often strip the emotionally available partner of her dignity. All the while, the emotionally unavailable partner acts like their partner deserves this treatment due to flaws in their character. It is an insidious and destructive process. The emotionally healthy person feels deeply hurt and angry due to the disrespectful and callous treatment but does not understand it because they trust their partner. So, the only conclusion is that their partner is right. That they are the flawed party in the relationship.

Unfortunately, because the emotionally unavailable person's attack is subversive and consistent, two things happen. First, the devaluing and disrespectful nature of the comments hurt the emotionally healthy person deeply. Secondly, the emotionally healthy person often ends up blaming himself because it is the only way to make sense of the situation without having to admit that their partner is toxic. This cycle erodes the emotionally healthy person's spirit. The essence of who they are is poisoned.

When a person's spirit suffers, a split is caused by the mind and the body. When a mind and body split occurs it causes anxiety, depression, and self-doubt. Unfortunately, all of these things lead the person to believe that it is them, and not their partner with the issues. At these times, one of the most important things to do is spend time away from the toxic partner. Also, engaging in mind and body activities will help the person get their spirit back. Once their spirit returns, they are more able to see the dysfunctional dynamic for what it is and free themselves.

An important distinction must be made, however. The difference between constructive criticism and a devaluing comment. It is a partner's responsibility to help their partner and provide awareness where it is lacking. Again, this sort of criticism is not a daily or weekly necessity, but nobody is perfect, and even the most insightful people have blind spots. It is a loved one's job to gently and supportively provide their partner with insight into an issue that might end up hurting them. Several examples will be presented to demonstrate the difference between constructive criticism and a devaluing statement.

Let's use Amy as the first example. Amy was a busy single mom who had a difficult time managing her large house and yard. There was a large trampoline in her yard that had been damaged by a storm. The netting was ripped in several places, and some of the poles were unstable. Amy didn't think much about it. She took the netting off and reminded her two seven-year-olds to be careful.

It was her partner that gently reminded her that other kids were jumping on the trampoline while she was not at home. Amy realized that someone could get badly hurt because often she was not home when the trampoline was being used. It was common for the neighborhood kids to run back and forth between yards. The danger and personal responsibility in this situation dawned on her. She immediately took the trampoline down. He stated, "Amy, that trampoline looks dangerous without a net. What happens when you are not home?"

Now let's review the feedback from a toxic partner. A toxic partner would say something like, "Are you crazy? Why do you have that death trap up? It is your fault if a kid gets hurt. You'll be sued for everything you have, and I won't be around to help you, so don't ask me!"

The first statement is respectful, and its intent is to protect Amy. The second statement is disrespectful, devaluing, blaming, and insinuates that Amy is crazy, stupid, incompetent, and a bad person. The difference is monumental. One intervention is healthy, and the other is abusive. In essence, a loved one should always look out for their partner, and help them gain insight through constructive criticism, but the criticism should always be respectful.

Ben provides another example. At the grocery store, he asked his two kids to pick out a drink to take to the pool, yet Ben was in a hurry and did not realize his daughter selected a drink in a glass container. When he picked up his partner, she casually mentioned this to Ben, quietly stating, "Honey, if Molly drops her drink, the glass might break and she might get hurt." Ben realized the danger and quickly found a fun pink water bottle to transfer the water into.

Yet a toxic person might say something like, "Oh my God, Does she have glass?! What are you thinking? You're an idiot. She's going to drop it and ruin everyone's time." The difference is obvious. One criticism is constructive and helpful, and the other is attacking and disrespectful.

In essence, an unavailable person sabotages their partner's identity, which detracts from the essence of who they are. This renders an emotionally healthy person damaged and unable to share their gifts with the world. Re-establishing the mind and body connection can help the person find their spirit again. When they feel whole, they are more equipped to stop the dysfunctional cycle.

Summary

E veryone seems plagued with anxiety and depression these days. The divorce rate is higher then 50%. Too many children are taking some sort of psychotropic medication by the time they are in middle school. Many married couples are not having regular sex. Why? Because the most important relationships in our lives have become distant. They lack emotional closeness, which means the joy, comfort, companionship, and chemistry once present is gone—replaced by loneliness, sadness, and frustration.

Often emotional closeness is lost because of a mismatch in emotional availability. One person in the partnership is emotionally evolved and one is not. Yet, there is help. Although the equation for emotional closeness is simple, it does require education, commitment, energy, and a desire to love and love well. Hopefully, this book has provided the education and motivation.

Accountability + Empathy = Emotional Closeness

For those on a quest to find a loving life partner, choose carefully. Emotionally unavailable people are difficult be with in a relationship, and their inadequacies not only impact you, but your future children. The ideas and examples in this book explain how to select an emotionally available partner.

Parents, the most important thing in your child's life is their relationship with you. Not much else matters. If there is emotional closeness, your child will not be anxious, depressed, or miserable. You will have more fun with your child and parenthood will be a joy instead of a struggle. So, stop working extra hours to pay for their new gadget and love them better. Love them well. Spend less money on them and love them better. The emotional investment is the most important investment of your life. Open your heart not your wallet.

Bibliography

Bazelton, E. *Sticks and Stones: Defeating the Culture of Bullying and Rediscovering the Power of Character and Empathy.* Random House. (2013).

Beckner, V., Arden, J. *Conquering Post Traumatic Stress Disorder.* Quailside Publishing Group. (2013).

Bion, W.R. *Attention and Interpretation.* Tavistock. London. 1970.

Bornstein, R. *The Dependent Personality Disorder.* Guilford Publications. New York. (1993).

Eigen, M. and Robbins, A. (1980). Object Relations and Expressive Symbolism: Some Structures and Functions of Expressive Therapy. In *Expressive Therapy,* Ed. A. Robbins, pp. 73–94. New York: Human Sciences.

Fraiberg, S., Adelson, E., and Shapiro, V. *Ghosts in the Nursery: A Psychoanalytic Approach to the Problems of Impaired Infant-Mother Relationships.* American Child Psychiatry. 14(3). 387–421. (1975).

Freud, S. (1914). On Narcissism: an Introduction. *Standard Edition* 14:73–102.

Gallwey, T. (1974). *The Inner Game of Tennis, The Classic Guide to the Mental Side of Peak Performance.*

Gervais, S. *Objectification and Dehumanization.* Nebraska. Springer. (2013).

Grotstein, James. *Splitting and Projective Identification.* Aronson. New York. (1977).

Kohlberg, Lawrence (1981). *Essays On Moral Development,* Vol. 1: *The Philosophy's of Moral Development.*

Bibliography

Kohut H, *Analysis of the Self.* New York. International Universities Press (1971).

Masterson, J., Francis, T. *The Narcissistic and Borderline Disorders: An Integrated Developmental Approach:* 18ᵗʰ Ed. New York. Routledge (1981).

Million T. *Personality Disorders and Modern Life.* John Wiley and Sons, Inc. New Jersey. (2007).

Ogden, Thomas. *Projective identification and the Psychotherapeutic Technique.* Rowman and Littlefield Publishers, Inc. Lanheim, (1991).

Samenow, S. *Inside the Criminal Mind.* New York. Random House. (2004).

Sheckler, C. Untitled article in the South Bend Tribune. Online. June 3, 2013.

Scharff, Jill. *Projective and Introjective Identification and the Use of the Therapists Self.* Aronson New York, (2004).

Spilluis, Elizabeth and O'Shaughnesy, Edna. *Projective Identification the Fate of a Concept.* New York. Routledge. (2012).

Summers, Frank. *Object Relations Theories and Psychopathology.* The Analytic Press. Hillsdale. 1994.

Winnicott, D. W. (1953). Transitional Objects and Transitional Phenomenon. *International Journal of Psycho-analysis* 34:89–97.

Young, R. *Racism: Projective Identification and Cultural Processes.* Process Press. London (1992).

About the Author

Dr. Erin Leonard has been a practicing psychotherapist for 15 years. Currently, she practices in Indiana with Dr. Sonego and Associates. During her time at Children's Memorial Medical Center, she was awarded the Shaw Research Award. She was recently a contributing expert to *Time.com* for a special feature on the 12 Worst Habits For Your Mental Health. Dr. Leonard has also appeared on WGN and FOX affiliates in Dallas, Boston, Memphis, Atlanta, and Phoenix.

Dr. Leonard graduated with her Master's degree from The University of Michigan, and her Doctoral degree, with a child and adolescent specialization, from The Institute of Clinical Social Work.

51625786R00085

Made in the USA
Lexington, KY
30 April 2016